J.K. LEVER

A CRICKETER'S CRICKETER

J. K. LEVER
A CRICKETER'S CRICKETER

J. K. LEVER AND PAT GIBSON
FOREWORD BY ALLAN BORDER

UNWIN HYMAN
London   Sydney   Wellington

First published in Great Britain
by the Trade Division of Unwin Hyman Limited, 1989

UNWIN HYMAN LIMITED
15–17 Broadwick Street
London W1V 1FP

Allen & Unwin Australia Pty Ltd
8 Napier Street, North Sydney, NSW 2060, Australia

Allen & Unwin New Zealand Pty Ltd with the Port Nicholson Press
Compusales Building, 75 Ghuznee Street, Wellington, New Zealand

British Library Cataloguing in Publication Data

Lever, J. K. (John Kenneth)
    J. K. Lever: a cricketer's cricketer.
    1. Cricket, Lever, J. K. (John Kenneth)
    I. Title II. Gibson, Pat
    796.35'8'0924
    ISBN 0–04–440438–7

Typeset in 12/14 Baskerville by Nene Phototypesetters Ltd, Northampton
and printed in Great Britain at the University Press, Cambridge

Contents

List of Illustrations

Foreword
by Allan Border

There must be a million stories about John Lever and at least one of them is printable . . .

A couple of years ago when I was with Essex we played Nottinghamshire in the quarter-final of one of the limited-overs competitions. It was an important match with plenty at stake and lots of tension on the field. Clive Rice punched a delivery from J.K. through point, ran the first run and dropped his bat at Lever's feet as he turned and scampered the second. J.K. picked it up, played a copybook forward defensive stroke as the ball was returned to him – his best shot for two years as far as anybody could remember – and we all enjoyed the light relief . . . except that the umpire added five runs to Rice's score and J.K. suddenly realised he had conceded seven off one delivery in a match where seven an over is too many. Even he struggled to see the funny side of that, and there is very little which does not appeal to John's sense of humour.

I did not really know what I was letting myself in for when I signed to play for Essex in 1986. They were a successful team with several good players. That much was obvious enough. But it was only after I signed up and word got around that people began making odd remarks.

I got the distinct impression that Essex had a reputation. Not to put too fine a point on it, they were broadly regarded as a team of nutters. I heard vague stories of men riding bicycles round the outfield; names like Keith Pont and Ray East began to conjure up visions of a different sort of men in white coats. But I was intrigued. And, frankly, I reckoned that after several seasons of solidly serious cricket I could do with playing in a different atmosphere.

Essex did a lot for me in that respect. Playing for them was therapeutic and nobody epitomised their approach to the game better than J. K. Lever.

In a sense, he represents what the club stands for. A lot of their success has been built around his bowling and the whole atmosphere of the place reflects his antics and attitudes.

John is a fantastic competitor. He loves to have the ball in his hand and to go out and bowl. In fact nobody does what he has done for twenty years and more without having a special love of the game. Some guys who bowl for a living consistently complain how hard it is to run in and bowl fast day after day. They may be right, but I cannot recall J.K. ever complaining. His reaction to the pressures and disappointments, the drudgery, I suppose, was always light-hearted.

I first caught a glimpse of him on England's tour of Australia in 1978–79. He did not play a lot on that trip but I have no doubt he was a leading member of the fines committee or the parties committee or whichever committee had the responsibility for lifting everybody's spirits. He is a magnificent tourist.

By the time I got to Essex in 1986, he had started to lose a bit of his zip as a bowler but he was still very competitive and very dangerous given the right conditions, and he still had the knack of getting people out.

His record over the years as a wicket-taker speaks for itself and it did not take too much imagination to visualise him as a young strapper doing an awful lot of damage in his heyday.

I am surprised he did not play more often for England. Perhaps his approach to the game did not impress the right people. I do not know. But if we had his sort of bowler achieving his success year in and year out in Australia I am sure we would have seen him in the Test side a bit more often.

John Lever represents a special sort of cricketer: a bloke who enjoys life to the full, who can find time to enjoy his cricket even when it is repetitive hard work and a real, deep-down professional. I do not suppose even he can go on for ever, but when he decides to call it a day Essex will lose a great character and professional cricket will be a little bit poorer.

There will always be the stories, of course. All 999,999 of them. I would hate to miss the book.

1

The Ilford Cockney

There are two large silver cups on the sideboard in my parents' home at Ilford in Essex which my father polishes with loving care and attention. They were presented by the Cricketers' Association, the professional organisation that represents every county cricketer in England, when they voted me their "player of the year" in both 1978 and 1979, and I think my father knows how much they mean to me.

I never wanted to be anything other than a cricketer from the age of about twelve when I realised that I was not going to be good enough to be a professional footballer. So to be honoured as the players' player, better still the cricketers' cricketer, in two successive years gave me a wonderful feeling of acceptance and a real sense of pride. My 106 first-class wickets in each of those seasons obviously had a lot to do with it, but I like to think that it also reflected the way I played the game.

The longer I have played – and I am now approaching my twenty-second season with Essex – the more I have come to appreciate that there is a right way and a wrong way to play cricket. The very thought that I got it right in the eyes of my fellow-professionals, my peers, when I was still relatively young and headstrong makes me appreciate my upbringing and my grounding in the game, which I am not sure that every young player gets these days.

I am not saying that my idea of the right way to play is necessarily the correct one, but if I ever become involved in managing or coaching youngsters I will insist that the etiquette of cricket is just as important as the play itself. I believe that if we ever lose sight of that we will lose a large part of the game and all it stands for.

There have been enormous changes during my career. Some of them have been all to the good and made the game far more professional, much better organised and even financially prosperous. Others, to be frank, I have found quite distasteful.

I am not too bothered about the bowlers who rant and rave and tell the batsman where to go when they get him out. After all, bowlers have always shouted their appeals *to* the umpire, although why they have to point and scream so ferociously *at* the umpire these days is beyond me.

In spite of that, I still do not think that there is too much verbal abuse in the game and what I am really concerned about is the far more subtle use of gamesmanship which has crept in. Batsmen who nick the ball to the wicketkeeper and do not walk when they know that they are out are symptomatic of a desire to win at all costs which is not helping anybody – least of all the umpires.

It was a reflection of the sharp practices which have gone on when a new regulation was introduced in county cricket in 1988 delaying the appearance of a substitute for five overs after a player had gone off in order to stop unscrupulous sides replacing an old and not so agile fielder with a younger, more fleet-footed one. It started in international cricket but it was the counties who had to suffer, even though we had not had too many problems with it. I am sure that the umpires would have been able to stamp it out if they had been given the authority to do so.

As it was, we saw some ridiculous situations – such as at the start of the Surrey innings against us in a Benson and Hedges Cup match at Chelmsford. Brian Hardie was in hospital, having his arm put in plaster after it had been broken by a ball from Sylvester Clarke, and Derek Pringle was in an adjoining ward for an X-ray on his wrist, which had been struck by the same bowler. Yet we were not allowed any substitutes for five overs, which makes a big difference at the start of a one-day innings because you cannot spare fielders to be in close catching positions.

I liked the comment of our scorer, Clem Driver, on the public address system when he announced: "Ladies and gentlemen, as you will see, five overs have now been bowled and Essex are sending on two more fielders just to make the game a little bit harder for Surrey."

That is an example of how cricket has definitely moved in the wrong direction. We can blame it on overseas players who may not be used to having umpires as good as ours and naturally try to get away with things now and again because they believe that it is all a bit of a lottery. We can blame it on the greatly increased prize-money in the game, which has made players more competitive and not averse to bending the rules a little. But, to me, both of them are pretty lame arguments and I do not like the trend.

In that respect, I am glad that I grew up in the game when I did – yet that does not mean that I do not wish that I was eighteen and starting all over again. It is only as you approach the end of your playing career and begin to think about finding another job that it really comes home to you how enjoyable it has all been. There has been no time during the past twenty-one years – whether I have been running around in the freezing cold or soaking wet of an English winter trying to get fit for the following season, or running in to bowl in temperatures of 100 degrees in the searing heat of India – when I would have wanted to do anything else.

I just cannot imagine any other job being equal to it – although I am well aware that, for every cricketer like me who can say that, there are dozens more who cannot. I have seen them putting in just as much time, just as much hard work and just as much practice as I have done – if not more. Yet they still have not got remotely near the pinnacles of playing for England at home and abroad, of winning the County Championship, of collecting a cup winners' medal at Lord's and, above all, of being chosen as a cricketer's cricketer.

No matter how hard you try, it still does not guarantee you a route into county cricket, a niche in a group of players who get on supremely well together and a part in a long-running success story. And, at the risk of sounding corny, I must say how lucky I have been to get all those things – lucky in my parents, lucky in my schools, lucky in my club and lucky in my county.

Wisden records that I was born at Ilford on 24 February 1949, but, for once, the cricketers' "bible" has got it wrong. In fact I was born at Stepney or, to be more precise, in the Whitechapel Hospital, because it was the time of the post-war baby boom and all the maternity homes in the Ilford area were full. Apparently my mother was very upset when she saw the birth certificate since there was a great deal of snobbery in those days and she thought some stigma might attach to the fact that I was born a Cockney. It was still there when I started playing cricket, too. The old school tie was very much in evidence and whenever anyone asked me where I was born I would say Ilford rather than Stepney.

It was not that we were a snobbish family. Far from it. My father was one of twelve children whose mother got him a job at the local butcher's shop when he was fourteen years old, and that put paid to any chance he had of ever becoming a cricketer. He had been quite a promising player at school and his teachers were keen for him to continue his education, but his mother had decided that it was time for him to get out to work and there was no arguing with that. The family came first.

I was more fortunate. My cricket ambitions did seem to come first and I have to admit that my sister, Linda, who is a year younger than me, suffered because of it. Throughout her childhood, she always had to play second fiddle to me and my sport and it was no surprise when she married at a very early age and escaped from the household.

Whether or not my dad was trying to achieve his own unfulfilled ambition through his son, I never knew. It was not an obsession with him and he did not push me into it. But he did have two jobs – following his trade as a butcher and working part-time as a decorator – and most of the extra cash went towards paying for my early days in cricket. We did not go away for too many holidays, apart from the odd week in a caravan at Bognor Regis.

Dad and mum would occasionally turn up to watch me play, although they always kept in the background and I never felt pampered. I travelled on public transport with my cricket bag, and while I am not suggesting that is how it should be today it does make some of us older players smile when we see so many parents driving their sons to the ground – and often carrying their bags for them as well!

My first experience of organised cricket had come while I was at Highlands Junior School where the headmaster, a Mr Cummings, was very enthusiastic about the game. We used to bat and bowl in the playground, and it was through the encouragement I got there that I went on to gain selection for the Ilford

Schools side at the age of ten – a year younger than the other boys in the team. The following year I took nine wickets for three runs in one game and was immediately pencilled-in for the next side up: Essex Under 15s.

Until then I had been keener on soccer than cricket. I was tall and skinny – about 6ft. with big feet and a 14in. neck – and used to captain the school football team from a kind of roving left-wing position where I could use my speed and shooting power. Then, as now, cricketers were poor relations compared with footballers, and my heroes were England and West Ham stars Bobby Moore, Geoff Hurst and Martin Peters, especially since they would come to Ilford once a year and play a fairly good game of cricket as well.

I was never quite as much of a West Ham fanatic as Graham Gooch – his dad used to take him to Upton Park as a boy with an orange box to stand on – because I preferred to play rather than watch, but I do remember cheering on the Hammers from the Wembley terraces when they beat Munich 2-0 in the 1965 European Cup Winners' Cup Final.

By then, though, my dreams of ever being a professional footballer had died in a district schools' trial match at the Cricklefield athletics stadium on the outskirts of Ilford. Trevor Brooking, later to play for West Ham and England, was among my opponents that day and suffice it to say that I felt a little bit out of my depth.

I continued to enjoy playing football, as well as badminton and tennis, but I concentrated hardest on my cricket and again I was in luck when I moved on to Dane County Secondary School and found two more masters who were only too keen to help me. It may sound trivial in the context of an international career, but those people who were prepared to give up some of their spare time to promote cricket were absolutely vital to my development. There are not so many of them around in schools these days and I think cricket is suffering because of it.

I was also fortunate to be living close to the famous Ilford Indoor Cricket School, which had been set up by Harold Faragher, a former captain of Ilford who had played a few games for Essex, with Trevor Bailey as its figurehead, and which was to prove a great investment for the future of Essex. Local schools went there for an hour once a week and we found ourselves being coached by Essex players of the time like Gordon Barker and Paddy Phelan as well as the resident coach, Bill Morris, who was to be the greatest single influence on my becoming a county cricketer.

William Bancroft Morris, born in Kingston, Jamaica, played only forty-eight matches for Essex between 1946 and 1950 as a middle-order batsman and spin bowler, but for me and a whole generation of young cricketers he was a giant of a man. I first got to know him when I was about eleven and for a while I was scared to death of him. He had a great, booming voice and a fearsome temper which would sometimes send schoolboys fleeing from the nets in tears.

I soon discovered, however, that it was only because he cared so much about the game. He would never lose his temper with them because they could not play but because they had been mucking about or not paying attention. If a boy showed promise or if he just showed that he was doing his best, Bill was always ready to slap him on the back. But if he thought that a boy had talent but was not prepared to make the most of it, he would kick him out of the school.

Bill was a stickler for discipline, appearance, good manners and doing things the right way – and that was before you actually started to play. Once you did, his coaching was that of a very correct, stylish player who left a lasting impression on me.

He never tired of talking about the game, but his method of coaching was not to bawl instructions down the net but to keep asking questions designed to make you think for yourself. He would watch me bowl at a batsman and say: "He's hitting you through midwicket. Now why do you think he's doing that?" Or: "He isn't having to play the ball on that line. What are you doing wrong?" And, by thinking about the answers to his questions, you immediately worked out for yourself that your length was wrong or your line was wrong and you had to do something about it.

He did not just teach me how to play cricket, either. I had always been fairly accurate and bowling left arm over seemed to be a great advantage because there were not too many people who did that. But he taught me that temperament was just as important as well by stressing the value of patience, and pointing out that if you could keep the batsman quiet for an over or two you could get him to make a mistake and hit the ball up in the air. Above all, I think he gave me an insight into what it was like to play cricket not just as a game but for a living and I will always be grateful to him for that.

Around that time, I also won a young fast bowlers' competition run by one of the London evening newspapers for which the prize was a winter's coaching at the even more famous Alf Gover Cricket School at Wandsworth. For months I trekked all the way across London via three underground stations every Sunday afternoon, but while I am sure it was a help I never learned as much there as I did from Bill, who was soon to give me another shove in the right direction.

During the winter, the Essex players used to have an indoor net at Ilford on Tuesday nights and, when I was about fourteen, Bill said: "Look, if you want to come along and have a bowl, there are always plenty of people who want to bat."

So there I was rubbing shoulders with some of the legends of Essex cricket and loving every moment of it. I just used to turn up in my plimsolls, bowl for an hour or two and then run all the way home. Bill was always there to keep an eye on me and make sure that my action was still up to scratch, and I really felt that I was somebody when I was invited to stay behind and indulge in the fish and chip suppers with which the players always ended the session.

By then I was sixteen and playing for the Ilford first team in what was a pretty high standard of club cricket. I sometimes wished that my dad could have been playing as well because there were plenty of other lads of my age whose fathers had worked their way up through the ranks. But although there were several occasions when he was close to putting on some whites he never actually did so.

Not that I was ever short of support and encouragement in that Ilford side. There was Bill Morris, of course, along with Harold Faragher, Roy Ralph, Peter Spicer and Ron Evans, who had all played for Essex. There was a Yorkshireman called Stuart Squires who bowled left-arm cutters and inswingers and gave me my first insight into the way Yorkshiremen play their cricket. "I'll have a slip and a gully," he would say. "Put the rest where you like." And then there was the captain, Ian Norton, who through my sixteen-year-old eyes at any rate, was good enough to play county cricket.

That is precisely what I intended to do when I left school, although my sports master wanted me to take up teaching and become a PE master. I had never worked hard enough academically to do that – I was far too busy playing cricket or soccer – and my exam results, three O-levels, reflected it. That did not worry me too much because apart from taking quite a few wickets for the premier club in the district, I had also been playing for

Essex Schools as well as for Essex themselves in second team, club and ground and young amateurs' matches under the coach, Frank Rist, who was forever picking me up and taking me here, there and everywhere.

With all that behind me, I was fairly confident that they would take me on the playing staff when I left school so it came as a bit of a shock when a contract was not immediately forthcoming. In the end I had to go to an employment agency in London to get myself a job. I found one as a clerk with a fire insurance company where I worked alongside a chap called Paddy Wilson, who had had a promising football career with Arsenal cut short by injury and who pointed out to me the pitfalls of being a professional sportsman. He did not put me off, though, and with Essex still keeping me waiting I wrote to Middlesex offering them my services.

I did not really want to play for Middlesex. I did not really believe that I could force Essex's hand. But I did know that if you wrote to another county, they had to obtain permission from the county of your birth before they could sign you and I thought it would be a good way of letting Essex know that I wanted to play cricket for a living.

Sure enough, I got a reply from Middlesex saying that they had inquired about my availability from Essex, who had said that they were not prepared to release me. And a few weeks after that I received a letter from Essex offering me a contract for the following summer at the princely sum of £500. For a lad from Ilford, I felt that I had been quite a crafty Cockney!

I needed just one more huge stroke of luck before I was on my way. While I was waiting to join the Essex staff I was involved in an accident when a van in which I was travelling with some friends left the road and hit a lamp-post. Two of us – one of the girls in the back and myself – went through the windscreen but while she, sadly, was in traction for months I escaped relatively unscathed, although it was terrifying at first as I lay flat on my back, unable to move.

It was sixteen years later before I discovered just how fortunate I had been. When I was in South Africa in 1982 I got a dreadful back pain which X-rays revealed was caused by a cracked vertebra, and I immediately thought to myself: "I think I know where that came from."

When I got back to England, the doctors suggested that I should have a similar operation to the one that my Essex colleague Neil Foster had at the age of twenty when they inserted two six-inch metal plates in his back. But I felt that I was too old to have such a major operation at thirty-three, and that if it had not bothered me for all those years then I might be able to get by for a little bit longer by working hard to build up my back muscles.

Little did I suspect that some of my best years were still ahead of me.

2

Tonker's Boys

One of life's great mysteries to me when I went to bowl at the county players in the Ilford Indoor School as a wide-eyed, hero-worshipping schoolboy was why Brian Taylor, the man who was to become captain of Essex, could always be found holding court afterwards wearing nothing but his socks and shoes. It was not until I reported to Chelmsford, on an April morning in 1967, to begin my career as a professional cricketer that I discovered the reason for such bizarre behaviour.

The County Ground was nothing like as well equipped as it is today and the facilities consisted of no more than two wooden sheds: one, where the shower was, for the senior players; the other, much more spartan and draughty, for the rest. And the first time you had to change in those sheds you realised that if you did not want to get splinters in your feet, you put your socks and shoes on first. It soon became a habit for most of us.

They were hard times for Essex. Trevor Bailey had arranged an interest-free loan through the generosity of the Warwickshire Supporters' Association to enable the county to buy the freehold of the ground, which he always says was the greatest single contribution he made to the club. But Essex were hardly a commercial proposition and money was still in short supply.

The playing staff had been slashed to twelve as part of the stringent economy measures and there were all kinds of fund-raising activities. One, I seem to recall, called on members to buy a nail to assist in the development programme, which seems a far cry from the "buy a brick" schemes you hear about these days. And at one stage, I was told, a committee man had to pay the players' wages for a couple of months because there was nothing in the bank.

The atmosphere was not the best, either. Trevor Bailey, having given up the secretary's job a year earlier, had just resigned and the choice of his successor had led to a good deal of bitterness. The choice was neither Barry Knight, the England all-rounder, who promptly resigned and went off to join Leicestershire, nor Gordon Barker, the Yorkshire-born opening batsman who had been Bailey's vice-captain and had naturally expected to take over. Instead the committee turned to Brian Taylor, a wicketkeeper and ferocious left-hand hitter who was known throughout the county circuit as "Tonker".

It proved to be an inspired appointment. There was no better turned-out cricketer than Tonker. His pads were always immaculate and he would only condescend to wear a sweater on the coldest days. There was no greater enthusiast for the game, either, and if he was anything at all to the younger players he was a father-figure. Naturally enough, we quickly became known as Tonker's boys.

In many ways he was more like a sergeant-major than a captain, a strict disciplinarian who would not tolerate any nonsense, and you soon learned how to stay on the right side of him. That was not too difficult for me after spending so much time under the influence of Bill Morris, and I never had any real problems. But for somebody like Ray East it was impossible, and he was always rubbing up Tonker the wrong way, much to the glee of the rest of us – especially Robin Hobbs, who would pick out the real gems and make them sound quite hilarious.

Raymond's clowning has been part of the Essex scene for as long as I can remember, but it could sometimes get him into deep water as it did one morning at Worcester. We could see Tonker getting redder and redder with rage as the session wore on because Raymond was not only fooling about but was also bowling so badly on a wicket that was turning a bit that in the end he did not want to bowl at all. And when we got back to the changing-room at lunchtime there was an air of expectancy as we waited for the explosion.

It was not long in coming. Tonker sat down, took his pads off and barked in his best military tones: "Raymond! Get your blazer on and see me outside!"

Raymond, eyes bulging, dutifully put on his blazer and did as he was told – but I do not know why they bothered to go outside. We could hear every word that was said as Tonker bellowed at him on the other side of the door.

When they came back in, Raymond apologised shamefacedly to the rest of the side for his behaviour and nothing more was said – until that evening. We were in the pub having a drink and every two minutes Hobbsy would leap to his feet and shout: "Raymond! Get your blazer on! I want to have a word with you outside."

That was typical of Hobbs. He never forgot anything and he was a good mimic as well, and that kind of thing did a lot to build up the spirit in the Essex side. It defused the situation and I think Raymond learned quite a lot from him so that in later years he himself became one of the better defusers of potentially ugly situations.

Hobbs occasionally got into trouble himself like he did one day when Tonker discovered that the club van was missing. "Well, where has it gone?" he demanded in some exasperation in the changing-room.

"I've lent it to Jackie Birkenshaw," confessed Hobbs, who saw absolutely nothing wrong in doing a favour to one of our Leicestershire opponents.

Tonker duly hit the roof, pointing out in no uncertain terms that he had no right to do such a thing. But, generally, he was a great admirer of Robin, who was a friend to everybody and a great team man – although, at first, I was a little bit wary of him. He was so sharp and quick-witted that I was not all that sure whether we were laughing together or whether he was laughing at me.

At least the club was not quite as university-orientated as it had been. The old "us" and "them" attitude between the senior players and the younger ones was still not too far away, but I never found it quite as pronounced as I might have done if I had started at Lord's, for instance. There, the "big three" of Peter Parfitt, Fred Titmus and John Murray may not have been to university but they were very much of the old school, and contemporaries of mine like Mike Smith and Clive Radley told me that if anyone stepped out of line at Lord's their feet would not touch the ground as they were shown the door.

I am not saying that there was anything wrong with that but we did certainly have to serve a tougher apprenticeship than youngsters do today. Even at Essex the junior players had to know their place and I must admit that I was scared stiff in those early weeks. I was familiar enough with even the most famous players – Bailey, Hobbs and Keith Fletcher (who were about to follow Trevor into the England side), Barker and his long-time opening partner Micky Bear – from all those net sessions at the Ilford school. But I had never even seen the first team play at Chelmsford and found the environment so strange that I just sat in the corner and did not dare to say two words to anybody.

In all honesty, there was no reason why I should have been so filled with awe. Pre-season training was nothing like as intensive as it is now – just a bit of fielding practice, a bat and a bowl if the nets were playable and, to try and get outselves fit, games of soccer enthusiastically led by Tonker, who had played professionally for Brentford. It was not too strenuous at all for a lad of eighteen but a far greater challenge was not far away.

Essex were desperately short of players and particularly bowlers. Trevor Bailey, in his last season, was to play in only eleven matches and when our opening bowler, Tony Jorden, the England rugby full-back, broke a knuckle I was pitched into the first team on 24 May 1967. The county had a policy of augmenting their slender playing resources by bringing in one or two club players on their home grounds – we were still playing at Brentwood, Leyton and Romford as well as Chelmsford, Colchester, Ilford and Westcliff – and, as luck would have it, I made my debut at Ilford in the middle of May.

That must have helped me because the run-up is so important to a bowler and I felt quite happy running up at Ilford as I had been doing week in and week out since I was fourteen. Valentine's Park does look – and indeed is – a completely different ground when the county is playing there with seats, tents and, in those days before advertising boards, a picket fence all the way found, but I was obviously more at home there and, consequently, less nervous than I would have been anywhere else.

Ron Evans winked at me and said: "I always knew you'd get there," and that seemed to be the general attitude at the club. But to me – and I am sure to my mother, sitting somewhere around the fence with her knitting, and my father, having a couple of pints in the tent that served as a public bar with his mates – it was not quite so run of the mill. And I will never forget a little boy of about six coming up to me at the end of the first day and asking for my autograph. I did not know where to put myself and hurriedly signed his scrap of paper before disappearing into the pavilion red-faced with embarrassment.

We were playing Worcestershire, and after we had been dismissed for 197 – J. Lever bowled d'Oliveira 7 – I opened the bowling with Keith Boyce and quickly took the wickets of Ron Headley and Alan Ormrod to help us gain a first-innings lead. We made only 129 in our second innings – J. Lever bowled Coldwell 0 – but when Worcester went in again needing 174 to win I had the biggest thrill of my young life by taking three more quick wickets, including that of the great Tom Graveney.

The odd ball was bouncing a bit and the occasional one stopping and Tom, who seemed to have decided to play a few shots, as they say, drove at a delivery slanting across him and was caught behind by Brian Taylor. As he nicked it, I turned and appealed to the umpire and Micky Bear, at mid off, came up and said: "I don't think I could have seen a bigger grin if I'd given you £500." Certainly it was a moment I will never forget.

The match was drawn – in fact we won only three of our twenty-eight matches in the championship that season to finish fifteenth – but I went on to play in thirteen games, taking twenty-six wickets at just over thirty runs each. It was not bad for a beginner and, more importantly, it had taught me my first vital lesson which was to stand me in good stead throughout my career.

I had not been the quickest bowler by any means when I first started playing at school, but from the age of about fifteen I had begun to think of myself as a fast bowler. Now I realised that I was not a fast bowler at all: I was a medium-fast or swing bowler. As a left armer bowling over the wicket, all I had been doing was pushing the ball across the right-handed batsman, bowling outswingers, as it were. It is the common fault of any left-handed youngster who tries to bowl too quick. The wrist turns over and away the ball goes towards the slips.

It was Arthur Milton, the old Gloucestershire and England opening batsman, who first brought that home to me in one of my earliest matches at Bristol. Every time I pitched the ball on the stumps, he would just run it down to third man; every time I pitched it outside leg to hit the stumps he simply clipped it down to fine leg. He was kind enough to have a little chat with me afterwards and explain where I was going wrong and I decided there and then that it would be back to the drawing-board at the end of the season.

I got more invaluable advice from Garry Sobers, who immediately struck me as one of the nicest blokes I had ever met as well as being the greatest cricketer I have ever seen. He sought me out to give me a few more tips on the art of left-arm swing bowling and, for the next two winters, I went back to the Ilford indoor school and Bill Morris.

He confirmed everything that I had been told. "Good effort getting those twenty-six wickets," he said, "but that average of thirty has got to come down to twenty-five. The inswinger is the ball that you must bowl. It's got to be your stock ball." And after that it became a habit for me to go into the net with a newish ball and, from three or four paces, just concentrate on trying to swing it in.

I have never lost that habit, either. I have always had to work at swinging the ball in because it has never come all that naturally to me. Even now, when I get tired, the ball will disappear across the batsman towards the slips. But in learning to bowl the inswinger as well it has given me the variety to move the ball both ways, and that is why I have taken so many more wickets towards the end of my career than I did at the beginning. I had learned that bowling as quick as you can does not get you as many wickets as the ability to manipulate the ball.

My forty-nine wickets in 1968 – when I played in twenty-five matches and helped Essex climb one place in the championship — still cost more than thirty runs apiece, and it was not until my third season that the future suddenly began to look infinitely brighter for both Essex and myself. The ever-generous Warwickshire Supporters' Association enabled the county to build a handsome new pavilion at Chelmsford, and my fifty-four wickets at 23.85 helped us rise to sixth in the championship. More important, though, was the fact that it was the first year of the John Player Sunday League, and it could not have come at a better time for us.

Gordon Barker was still playing, but basically we were a young, fit and highly enthusiastic side with Tonker, as ever, leading from the front. Whereas Lancashire, the dominant side in one-day cricket at the time, had Harry Pilling as their anchor-man, just nudging and working the ball around and generally holding things together, we had Tonker. He would go in first (without a helmet, of course), and without any thought for himself and just smack the ball around the way he knew best.

On his day, he really could tear an attack apart and I still have vivid memories of a match at Leicester where that great Australian fast bowler Graham McKenzie was bowling pretty quickly on a bouncy pitch. Tonker wandered out there and smashed fifty off the first five overs, including one incredible hook when the ball flew off the top edge over the wicketkeeper's head and embedded itself in the sight-screen. Play was delayed while they climbed up to get the ball out.

It was a fairly typical Tonker innings. He would get to forty or fifty and then, as soon as a spinner came on, he would smack the ball straight down somebody's throat in the deep. Back he would come into the changing-room and say: "Oh, if only I could have had a bit of luck." And the players who had all been watching the situation and had seen the spinner come on and the fielder take up his position would look at one another knowingly.

Still it was quite successful. Even if we then lost a few more wickets and ran into a sticky patch, there were still enough overs left for lesser batsmen to push the ball around and give us a total we were capable of defending. Our strength was in our bowling and in our fielding – and in the presence of Keith Boyce, who did more than anyone else to make Essex an attractive, even fashionable side.

Trevor Bailey, to whom Essex owed so much in those days, came across Keith Boyce while he was captaining the Rothmans Cavaliers in Barbados and promptly signed him on. He had to spend a year's qualification period in the second team and that was where I got to know him. My first room-mate had been Roland Kilby, a wicketkeeper-batsman who played for the Metropolitan Police before joining Ilford and used to look after me. But from the time I got into the first team until he left the club I always roomed with "Boycey".

We were together for ten years and though it was not always easy watching him smoke twenty cigerettes a night, not being a smoker myself, I admired the bloke tremendously. It was not so much because of his cricketing brain, especially in the early days when he was very green and most of our opponents would be taken aback by the sight of this young West Indian who would smack the ball miles, try to knock batsmen's heads off with his genuinely quick and hostile bowling and then run around the boundary, pick up the ball one-handed and rifle it back over the top of the stumps, threatening to leave a bullet-hole in anybody who got in the way. But his attitude was fantastic. Brian Taylor, who would drive the club van just because it had "Essex" on the side, was Essex through and through. Keith Fletcher, who always insisted that it was not personal performances but the team performance that mattered, was Essex through and through. And Keith Boyce was Essex through and through from the day he arrived in England to play for Walthamstow and bought a house there. He was not like an overseas player. He was one of us.

He is six years older than me and I often felt that he was protective towards me, on the field as well as off it. He was always there with a few words of encouragement, but I think I gained most from the example he set. He gave 110 per cent every time he stepped on to the field and he gave it from the word "go". While everyone else was trying to get loose in a morning, there he was, all loose-limbed anyway, bowling his first ball at lightning speed.

Once he hit dear old Arthur Milton in the chest with a ball that bounced a bit more than he expected and down he went in a heap, groaning: "Oh, Boycey, what have you done to me here?" And Boycey was the first man there to help him to his feet and make sure that he was all right.

David Shepherd, another Gloucestershire batsman, was also a memorable victim of Boyce's aggression, though in rather less painful circumstances. He decided to risk one for the throw against Boyce, all of eighty or ninety yards away on the distant boundary, only to be overtaken halfway through his second run by what looked like an Exocet as the ball screamed over his shoulder and thudded into Brian Taylor's gloves.

"Oh God," muttered the perspiring "Shep", now a familiar rotund figure as a Test match umpire and never the most nimble runner between the stumps, "I got that a bit wrong, didn't I."

Aggression was also the name of Boyce's batting and that could have hilarious results, too. Once we were trying to block for a draw when, having hit one ball over the pavilion, he ran down the wicket to the next and tried to do it again and was stumped by a mile.

"What do you think you were doing?" we asked him when he got back to the changing-room.

"Well," he explained, "I thought if I kept hitting it over the pavilion it would waste a bit of time."

That was Boycey, a cricketer who could hit the ball harder, bowl it quicker and throw it further than anybody else in our side. And if I have one regret it is that Essex did not manage to win anything while he was with the club.

I know that he was acutely disappointed that most of the other West Indians who came into English cricket around the same time as he did finished up winning things with their counties, and he must have been heart-broken that his career ended in the way that it did in 1977. He had such a bad knee injury that even the top surgeons could not do anything about it.

His benefit brought him scant consolation. It was not as well organised as benefits are now and he was spending more in the pubs than he was getting from the bat raffles. He went back to Barbados with only a few pounds to his name and no job to go to and tragically finished up with a drink problem.

The first time I went out to the Caribbean and tried to look him up he did not want to see anybody. The next time he did agree to see me but he was not the Boycey that I remembered. I recall thinking at the time that things might have been different if he had stayed in England and I felt sad that we had not done more to keep him here, so I was delighted when he turned up again at Chelmsford in the summer of 1988 looking much more like his old self. He had got himself a new girlfriend; his daughter, now in her twenties, was about to be married; and he was even talking about playing a bit of cricket with the youngsters. I just hope that he is as much of an inspiration to them as he was to us in that first Sunday League season.

We invariably batted under pressure, often in a state of panic and sometimes fairly abysmally. But we bowled reasonably well and our fielding took us into third place by winning us more matches than I can remember.

Fielding was our forté, and that was wholly due to Keith Boyce who was head and shoulders above anyone else around when it came to racing round the boundary, picking the ball up in one hand and returning it with a flat, fast, accurate throw.

The rest of us took our cue from him and from 1969 until Refuge Assurance took over the league in 1987 we won no fewer than nine medals for finishing in one of the top three positions. It was to be a long time before we actually won it, or anything else, come to that, but the confidence we acquired and the support that we were building up through our Sunday performances were beginning to rub off in the other competitions.

Essex were as close as they had ever been to winning a title in 1971 when we were runners-up to Worcestershire in the John Player and narrowly beaten by Lancashire, the eventual winners, in the third round of the Gillette Cup, but we still tended to panic when we were chasing runs and found it almost impossible to win batting second. And it was not really until after Brian Taylor retired in 1973, Keith Fletcher took over the captaincy and, to a certain extent, Mike Denness arrived from Kent to bring a calming influence to the batting that we became serious and consistent challengers for the game's top honours.

But Tonker had sown the seed. A whole team – Fletcher himself, Robin Hobbs, Brian Edmeades, Keith Boyce, Ray East, David Acfield, Graham Saville, Stuart Turner, Brian Ward, myself and Neil Smith (in order of winning our county caps) – had grown up under him. And Fletcher was to reap the harvest.

3

Fletcher's Men

The first thing that you should know about Keith Fletcher is that he is tough. Very tough. There were plenty of people who wondered how this painfully shy, fairly diminutive country boy from Cambridgeshire could ever take over from such a pugnacious Cockney character as Brian Taylor. What they did not know was that he was very much his own man who had worked his way up from village cricket to Test cricket by thinking about the basics and sorting out the best way of playing the game – and he was about to apply the same principles to the task of captaining Essex.

It was no surprise to any of the players when he was given the job. I had not noticed it at the start because when I was not bowling I was invariably fielding on the boundary so I did not hear a lot of the conversations that went on between Taylor and Fletcher, standing alongside him at first slip. But I soon discovered that Keith was forever chipping in with advice about bowling changes or field placings and, as he grew in confidence and experience through playing Test cricket, he asserted more and more control.

If you talk to him now, Fletcher will admit that it was

1. My great mentor, Bill Morris, was captain of this Ilford side in 1966. Left to right: *back*, Harry Finn, Reg Whitehead, Alan Tack, Bill Bateman, JKL, Richard Carr, Horry Coyle (scorer); *front*, Stuart Squires, John Barr, Bill Morris, Ron Evans, Roy Fisher. (*E. W. S. Byers*)

2. Two of Tonker Taylor's boys who were to be major influences on my career – Keith Boyce, feeling the cold on arrival from Barbados, and the newly capped Keith Fletcher.

3. My first day as a professional cricketer in April
1967 ... bowling in the nets at Chelmsford with those old wooden
changing-rooms in the background. (*Central Press*)

4. Ray East leaps goalkeeper-style to beat me to the ball during pre-season fielding practice as the new Chelmsford pavilion takes shape in 1970. Also in the picture are Keith Fletcher, Eddie Presland, Stuart Turner, David Acfield and Robin Hobbs.
(*Sport & General*)

5. A "cricketers' cricketer". One of the proudest moments of my life as I receive the Cricketers' Association trophy from Trevor Bailey, a man who did so much for Essex cricket.

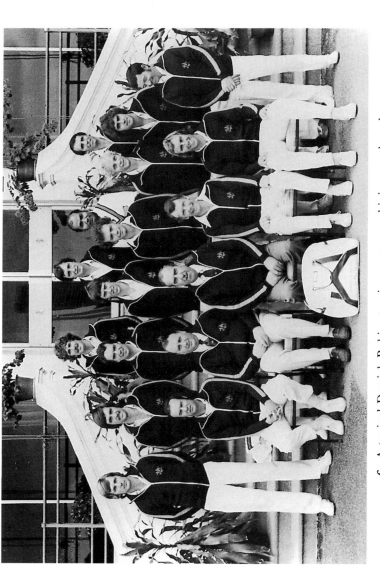

6. A typical Derrick Robins touring party, combining youth and experience. Left to right: *back*, John Wright, John Emburey, Intikhab Alam, Roger Tolchard; *middle*, Geoff Howarth, Peter Willey, Phil Carrick, David Gurr, Kevin Jarvis, David Gower, Chris Cowdrey, Harry Pilling; *front*, Mike Smith, Joe Lister (manager), Derrick Robins, Mike Denness (captain), JKL.

not a particularly good idea to make him captain when he was playing regularly for England. He does not think that you can do the job properly when you are away so often and do not know what your players have been doing from day to day. He had a seasoned and knowledgeable deputy in Robin Hobbs, but I do believe that we suffered from Fletcher's lengthy absences during his first season in charge. In fact, the battering he got from Dennis Lillee and Jeff Thomson in Australia in 1974–75 that took away much of his appetite for Test cricket was a blessing in disguise for Essex. I think we would have won something before 1979 if we had had the stability we got when he dropped out of the England side.

He never worried half as much about his own performances when he was playing for Essex as he had done when he was playing for England – and that was how he transmitted his love for the county and his devotion to the cause to the rest of us. He simply would not stand for anybody playing for himself and not pulling his weight for the rest of the side, and that created an environment in which everybody felt happy and secure. The batsmen could go out and have a slog if we were chasing an impossible target knowing that failure would not be held against them. The bowlers knew that if they had a lean time the threat of the axe would not be hanging over them.

The longer he stayed in the job, the more we felt that he had the full support of the committee and we could relax in the knowledge that if it came to the crunch at the end of the season he would stand up for any one of us and say: "You're not getting rid of him."

In all the years that I have played under him, I cannot think of one single player who got into the first team and was not given every opportunity to prove himself. There may have been one or two unlucky second team players who never got a chance at all so we never really found out how good they were, but anybody who did play for the first team could always rely on the captain's one hundred per cent support.

It all produced a camaraderie, a feeling of together-ness, an atmosphere in the changing-room that was probably just as important to the end product as Fletcher's tactical skills on the field. We had all grown up together so we could say anything we liked to each other – and we very often did. There was not much talking behind anyone's back. With people like Ray East, Stuart Turner and David Acfield around, things tend to come out and if there were any grievances they were all aired.

When you are virtually living together for three or four months of the year, there are bound to be a few problems. There must be times when you get on each other's nerves. But there was just something about the Essex changing-room that was rather special. We got our problems out of the way ourselves. No one went outside and moaned to anybody else. And I would not have wanted to play my cricket any other way.

It was all done with humour, of course, because humour was never very far away. Robin Hobbs was the greatest leg-puller I have every met, and if Ray East was our clown prince then Keith Pont was a worthy successor when he joined the side.

East was responsible for giving Keith Fletcher a couple of his nicknames. The first I remember was "Wilf", which dated back to the days when we used to play in a few benefit football matches and Keith in his baggy shorts hanging round his knees reminded everyone of one of those old-time footballers like Wilf Mannion. The other, of course, was "Gnome" – apparently because Raymond thought that a pair of those old winkle-picker shoes that Keith wore until the toes turned upwards made it look as though he had fallen off a toadstool!

It did not take Pont long to follow in that tradition. In

one of his first matches under Brian Taylor he had to field at third man at one end and fine leg at the other, so he borrowed a bicycle from a boy in the crowd and pedalled his way round the outfield at the end of the over while the rest of us fell about laughing.

There was so much hilarity at times that Ray Illingworth was once quoted as saying: "That bunch of madmen will never win anything."

But he was wrong for the simple reason that Fletcher would never let it get out of hand. He has a nice dry sense of humour himself – though I did not really find out about it until I went on an England tour with him – and probably appreciated its value. There are times when you do feel down after losing a match but you can get so far down that you cannot get back up again. If we won, we celebrated. If we lost, we finally swallowed our disappointment and had a laugh.

I thought it was a great tribute to the Essex attitude when Robin Hobbs, who had retired in 1975, made a comeback four years later as captain of Glamorgan. Tony Lewis said that the reason why they had appointed him was that while they had some good cricketers in Glamorgan they did not seem to be getting anywhere so they wanted somebody in charge who would at least help them to enjoy their cricket. I do not know whether it worked, but it was nice to think that they had looked around and found somebody from our changing-room to do that for them.

I suppose it worked for us because the chemistry was just right – although we were strange bedfellows in many ways. Apart from the Barbadian Boyce and the local boy Lever, the rustic Ray East shared with the studious Cambridge Blue and Olympic fencer David Acfield; Stuart Turner, reared in Essex club cricket, struck up an immediate rapport with Brian Hardie, a Scot from Stenhousemuir; Keith Pont practised his jokes on Neil

Smith, as easy-going a Yorkshireman as you could ever meet; and Graham Gooch, an apprentice tool-maker from Leyton, teamed up straightaway with Ken McEwan, a South African farmer's son who had followed Lee Irvine, another South African, and Australian Bruce Francis as our overseas batsman.

Ken McEwan, in particular, must have found it all a bit bewildering at first. One of his earliest matches for Essex was a friendly in Scotland where Ken – still a single man in those days, I hasten to add – met a young lady on the hotel dance-floor. He was escorting her from the room when he came face to face with her boyfriend, who promptly punched him in the face, knocked him to the floor and kicked him about the head.

Ken turned up for breakfast the next morning with bumps and bruises all over his face, his eyes and lips sore and swollen, and one of our committee-men turned to him and said: "Was he a particularly nasty sort of chap, this fellow who you bumped into last night?"

McEwan looked at him, wondering what kind of set-up he had joined – and we looked at McEwan's battered face wondering what we had been lumbered with. But none of us need have worried. Because he was a South African and never got the chance to play at the highest level, Essex supporters will forever argue about how good a player he really was. But having seen him play on all kinds of pitches – with him in England, against him in South Africa – I know what a good player he was.

I used to feel very sorry for him when he saw his best mate, Graham Gooch, going off to play Test cricket and enjoying all the trappings of success while he was forced to remain as just an ordinary county cricketer. And looking back on his career, I wonder whether he should have tried to become eligible for England like Allan Lamb and the Smith brothers, Chris and Robin, did. Certainly I think he was every bit as good as them. But he always said that he was happy to stay as he was and we were happy to have him because his continuous presence obviously made us a better side.

While he was a quiet lad and never seemed to be too ambitious, his attitude to batting and his views on cricket were always very positive and sensible. He would rarely volunteer anything, but if one of the other batsmen wanted to sit down and talk to him he would come out with what I always felt was the right kind of advice.

Most of the time, though, he was content to offer a few well-chosen words to get Ray East or Keith Pont on the right wavelength and then sit back and giggle quietly at the banter that followed. I think he was a bit taken aback when Chris Gladwin came into the side and, with the audacity that youngsters seem to have these days, started calling him "Spam Head" or "Chrome Dome" because of his thinning hair. Ken could hardly believe that a junior player could talk to one of his seniors like that, but generally he took it well and did not get too upset.

Another "import" who slotted quickly into the Essex scheme of things was Brian Hardie, who became so inseparable from Stuart Turner that we used to call them "Tweedledum and Tweedledee".

By then Stuart was firmly established as a vital member of the side but he had not found it so easy to begin with. After his first season on the staff in 1965, he received a note through his door informing him that his services were no longer required, which was fairly shabby treatment by Essex's standards today. Back he went into club cricket where he worked so hard at his game and showed such a competitive spirit that Essex admitted their mistake and took him back again.

With only twelve players on the staff at the time, there was no way that they could overlook Stuart's ability any longer and he rapidly developed into a very fine cricketer indeed – though not without the odd jarring setback. He had still not worked out the quicker bowlers all that well and one day at Leicester he got on to the back foot against a big, dark-haired paceman called John Cotton and was hit flush on the side of the face. Down he went and they carried him off.

Back in the dressing-room, he was lying on the table with a swelling the size of a duck's egg on his jaw when Tonker went across and said: "What's the matter with you, then? There's nothing wrong. Get back out there!"

At the fall of the next wicket, Stuart reeled his way back out to the middle and got on to the back foot again to the very next ball – which reared up at him, smashed into his glove and broke his thumb!

With that sort of encouragement he really did have to work hard at his batting, and it says a lot for his courage and commitment that towards the end of his career I saw him take on the very best fast bowlers like Wayne Daniel with his own individualistic brand of scoring shots.

As far as his bowling was concerned, he was like a machine. You just had to plug him in, adjust him to the right line and length and off he went. He was always steady, always accurate, always doing something with the ball – and I am not just talking about picking the seam! One or two counties called him "The Whistler" in his early days because he had a habit of running his thumb nail around the seam and you could hear it whistle as it went through the air.

Unfortunately, machines eventually wear out and, like one or two of us who have bowled long spells over the years – and they were particularly common at Essex – Stuart found that they had taken their toll. He used to get strapped up with knee braces and suchlike just to get himself out on to the field, but it must still have been a terrible wrench for him when he eventually had to admit: "I can't do it any more day in and day out."

It is a shame that you cannot come out of professional

sport the way you go into it from a fitness point of view, but it was typical of Stuart's competitive spirit that he still was not ready to pack up altogether. He went off to play for Cambridgeshire and become probably the best bowler in the Minor Counties where at least he had a week to recover from his exertions, although even that must have been very hard for him.

Whatever other qualities Stuart and Brian Hardie had in common, competitive spirit was certainly one of them because we did not think that "Lager", as we call him, could hit the ball off the square when he first joined us from Scotland, where he had made a few centuries against first-class opposition. In fact his first claim to fame – or was it infamy? – was his performace against Hampshire at Chelmsford in 1974 when he scored four runs in 142 minutes, the slowest innings in the county's history.

But he turned out to be a bit like Glenn Turner, that prolific New Zealander who started off as a blocker but worked out his own way of playing. Brian's method is not orthodox, it is purely something that suits him, and it has neither the easy elegance of Tom Graveney nor the bristling belligerence of Mike Gatting. But it has brought him thousands of runs and earned him respect throughout the county circuit.

On top of that he has contributed enormously to the all-round success of the side through his sheer guts in fielding for years in the suicidal bat-pad position at short leg where his helmet could not save him from being hit on every other part of the body. He also took some brilliant catches, not least off me. Being an inswing bowler, I obviously needed someone to field there a lot of the time and Brian is one of the best bat-padders I have ever seen.

If Stuart Turner and Brian Hardie typified the attitude of the Essex side in those days, then so, too, did Neil Smith and Keith Pont – although I hope they will not mind me saying that they both could have done with a bit more of the determination and will to win of the other two.

My lasting memory of Neil is of him sitting in a bar next to Ken McEwan with a pint of lager in one hand, a cigar in the other, a peppermint in his mouth and a big grin on his face listening to whoever was doing the wise-cracking at the time. Yorkshiremen are supposed to be dour and serious but Neil was quite the opposite and I suppose it was his inability to knuckle down and lose a bit of weight that eventually cost him his place in the side. But he was a more than useful player who was good enough to open the batting on occasions and took some stunning catches after taking over the wicketkeeping gloves from Brian Taylor.

Keith Pont, too, could have done to have worked a little bit harder at his game, especially his bowling, although he did a good all-round job for us, contributed enormously to some important victories and could prob-ably consider himself unlucky not to have played more than he did. There were a few occasions when he scored a hundred and was then dropped for the very next game, which is not very easy for anyone to take. Yet I know he would always say: "I'd rather have done what I did for Essex than play three times as many matches in a lesser side."

And then there were David Acfield and Ray East, "Ackers" and "Easty", the unlikeliest bedfellows of all. They had nothing whatever in common apart from the fact that they were both spin bowlers who could consider themselves unfortunate never to have played for Eng-land. It is probably the only thing they would ever agree about. They argued about everything else from the moment they got up in a morning until they went to bed at night – and, for all I know, they did not stop then because they always roomed together. It all seemed very

strange to the rest of us, but they really did seem to keep
each other going in what was a real love-hate relation-
ship.

"I bowled at the wrong end today," Acfield would say
in that educated voice that has become well known to
television viewers. "Oh no you didn't," East would reply
like the true comedian that he was. And off they would go
long into the night much to the amusement and amaze-
ment of the assembled company.

I am not sure whether they were always serious on
those occasions but they were in deadly earnest when
they argued about field placings. When they were
bowling, Acfield liked to put the pressure on by stopping
the batsman scoring runs while East used to do it by
having lots of fielders round the bat. But it always
annoyed East that Acfield could always have a man out
on the boundary for the slog yet when he asked for one,
the captain would say: "No. You're bowling to this field."
That was a real bone of contention between them for
years.

What was inarguable, however, was that both were
very fine bowlers. East actually played in two Test trials –
and did the hat-trick in one of them – and was obviously
unlucky in that there were so many other slow left armers
around at that time. There were Derek Underwood,
Phillippe Edmonds and Norman Gifford, and it must
have been very disheartening for him to think that no
matter how well he bowled he would have to wait for
them to be injured before he would get a chance.
Unfortunately, it never came.

As for Acfield, I think he was very under-rated. He was
a genuine, top-class off spinner in county cricket, but
again there were other such specialists around like John
Emburey, Geoff Miller, Pat Pocock and Eddie Hemmings. And the fact that most of them could bat rather
better than Acfield did, always came into it. I could

sympathise with him because I did not think that bowlers should necessarily be picked because of the brittleness of the batting – probably because I suffered in that respect myself.

There was just one problem in having two spinners of such quality. Robin Hobbs was still vice-captain and with three spinners in the side it was not very well balanced. For a while Acfield was still an amateur because of his Olympic fencing and he solved the problem by taking a couple of summers off to pursue his other sport. But when Keith Fletcher took over the captaincy it was a real dilemma and he showed his toughness in the way that he solved it – by leaving out his vice-captain, who promptly decided to retire.

As I have said, Brian Taylor was a great fan of Robin's and would not allow anybody to say a word against him. "Best leg-spinner in England," he would say, as though the fact that he was probably the only leg-spinner in England at the time had nothing to do with it.

There was a lovely moment in a Scarborough Festival match when Ashok Mankad, son of the great Vinoo, was batting and Robin was entertaining the crowd by tossing the ball higher and higher in the hope that the batsman would slog it up in the air. Ashok, who never did quite reach the heights of his father but still played in twenty-two Tests, kept reaching a long way forward and pushing each delivery back down the wicket.

In the end, he turned round ·to Tonker, shaking his head sadly, and said: "I am sorry but I cannot play this. It is not first-class bowling."

"I wouldn't worry about it, son," came back Tonker, sharp as a razor. "You're not a first-class player."

Be that as it may, Robin certainly was a first-class cricketer, a brilliant fielder and a skilful leg-spinner who took more than 1,000 wickets and went on four England tours. He also scored a century in forty-four minutes against the Australians at Chelmsford in his last season with Essex, but I think he would admit that he could only have played for us longer if he had been capable of batting higher up the order.

The decision to leave him out did not go down too well with Ray East, though. It left Acfield and myself as the only two players without any real pretensions as batsmen – and Raymond very much in the firing-line. For all that he liked to play the fool when he went in to bat – and I have seen him march out there and take up his position alongside the non-striker when a fast bowler was in full cry! – he was more than capable of scoring a few runs and the other sides knew it. And suddenly he was being bounced by every fast bowler in the land.

"They won't bounce you," he would say to me, "because you can give them a bit back. But they'll bounce the poor old slow left armer."

He did have a point. I remember one particular day at Bristol, where Mike Procter always got loads of wickets against us. Once more we were up against it and losing easily when I went out to bat with Raymond at the striker's end. And I could only feel sorry for my partner when Procter came steaming in and let fly a bouncer which clipped his nose as he took desperate evasive action.

It made a sound like a nick off the edge of the bat and all the close fielders went up in a concerted appeal with Sadiq Mohammad at short leg making more noise than the rest of them put together in true Pakistan tradition.

As Procter followed through half way down the pitch, Sadiq was still leaping up and down screaming: "He's hit it, he's hit it . . . and he's not walking!"

To which a shaken and definitely stirred Raymond replied: "I haven't hit it, you little shit. It's hit me on the f——g nose!"

"What did he say to you," demanded Procter.

"He's swearing at me ... he's swearing at me," wailed Sadiq.

By now Raymond was clutching his nose as though that was the only thing that was stopping it from falling off and eventually Procter accepted that he was telling the truth and eased off a little bit.

It was a fact that Procter usually did roar in against Essex and that poor old Raymond often seemed to be on the tail-end of it. But it was not just because he was a slow left armer. It was because his batting had improved immeasurably, his reputation had preceded him and bowlers knew that they had to get him out before he got too many runs.

So there we were. Fletcher had got his balanced side – an attack comprising Boyce, myself, Turner, East and Acfield with Pont in support, batsmen of the quality of Gooch, McEwan, Hardie and himself, all-rounders like Boyce and Turner and a wicketkeeper-batsman in Smith – yet still we could not win anything. We knew we were good players, we knew we were a good team, we knew we were well led, but, try as we might, we just could not get our hands on a trophy.

The John Player League still seemed to be our best bet. But having lost out to Worcestershire in 1971 by 0.0037 of a run per over when we finished joint top, we were pipped again in 1976 and 1977 under two different kinds of ruling, first by Kent on run-rate and then by Leicestershire because they had one more win than we did.

The following season was even more frustrating. For once we were not challenging for the Sunday League but we did finish second to Kent in the County Championship – our highest position ever – and reached the semi-final of the Gillette Cup for the first time only to lose to Somerset by the closest possible margin. I had to hit three off the last ball for victory, but Brian Rose's throw just beat Neil Smith's despairing dive and we were beaten with the scores level because Somerset had lost fewer wickets.

By then we were really beginning to believe that we were destined never to win anything. It is very hard to explain to anybody who has not experienced that sort of thing, but the psychological side of the game can be very powerful and the doubt and fear that used to creep into the side whenever we got into winning positions was something that we just had to eliminate.

Mike Denness, I firmly believe, was the man who helped us to do it. He had arrived from Kent in 1977, the year that we lost Keith Boyce, although Keith's untimely departure did not turn out to be as damaging as we all feared. In Boyce's place we got Norbert Phillip, a virtual unknown from Dominica in the Windward Islands, and he really did take us all by surprise. He was not as sociable as Boyce and, as a side, we found it hard to accept him at first, but he won us over by his performances and in the end he fitted in very well indeed. He had had very little coaching and did not even bother to measure out his run-up, just tossing the marker down somewhere near where he thought it should be. But he could be a very lively bowler indeed and loved to hit the ball just like Boyce did.

Yet for all Norbert's contribution, I think it was Denness who made the biggest difference in the side. The only place we could find for him to bat was as an opener, and I do not think he was too keen on that, but Fletcher's persuasive powers got him to do it for the good of the side – and that is just what it turned out to be. It was very much a short-term measure, but Mike was exactly what we needed at the time.

He had been a winner, you see, leading Kent to the John Player League title three times, the Benson and Hedges Cup twice and the Gillette Cup once. And none of us had the experience of winning.

4

The Breakthrough

The breakthrough came, at last, in 1979. After 103 years of trying – or twelve on my part – Essex finally won the County Championship. Yet the day we did it, Tuesday 21 August, turned out to be the biggest anti-climax I have ever known.

The only way we were ever going to win anything, I suppose, was to get so far ahead of everybody else that we just could not be caught whether we panicked or froze or simply lost our way – and that is precisely what we did. We hit the front on 18 May when we beat Derbyshire by an innings and 171 runs at Chesterfield and steadily drew further and further away, clinching the title with four matches still left and finishing a staggering seventy-seven points ahead of our closest challengers, Worcestershire.

Some churlish souls complained that we were lucky to have been able to play when other sides were being rained off. I dare say we were on one or two occasions, but they could hardly argue with our record of thirteen victories, five of them by an innings, compared with Worcestershire's seven. Despite losing Graham Gooch to the Prudential World Cup and four Test matches against India for more than half of the championship games, we usually collected maximum batting points with Ken McEwan, Mike Denness, Keith Fletcher and Brian Hardie all scoring more than 1,000 runs. And we just kept on bowling sides out.

Every single one of the bowlers played their part. Nobby Phillip finished with seventy first-class wickets. Stuart Turner had fifty-seven to set alongside his 500 runs despite the strain of running his benefit season. David Acfield (thirty-nine wickets) and Ray East (forty-three) bowled us to some crucial victories on the rare occasions when the conditions helped them. And I went through one of those rare periods in your life when you feel as though you can do nothing wrong.

In statistical terms, I took 106 wickets in the season, including five or more in an innings eight times. In successive matches at Chelmsford and Edgbaston I took twenty-six wickets, 13 for 117 against Leicestershire and 13 for 87 against Warwickshire. And in the month of June alone, I picked up fifty-three wickets.

Some people interpreted it as my answer to the England selectors who had left me out of the World Cup squad but, even if it had been, I wonder whether they even noticed. With the World Cup getting all the headlines, county cricket was relegated to the inside pages of the newspapers. We used to have a bit of a laugh about it over breakfast when somebody would say: "Oh, well bowled . . . I see you've got a mention alongside the greyhound results!"

The more likely reason was the climatic conditions that summer, especially in June. It was one of those months that was perfect for my type of bowling, so much so that I can remember switching on the television at home one evening and hearing the weather forecaster say: "It's going to be quite hot and humid again tomorrow and the way John Lever is going I'm sure he's going to enjoy another game for Essex in this weather."

I could hardly believe my ears as I sat there staring at the screen, but the weather gods really did seem to be with me. Every time I ran up to bowl the conditions seemed to be in my favour. It just happened like that. There was never too much wind and the ball would swing around nicely in the humid atmosphere.

But there were valid cricketing reasons for our success as well. Because we had scored lots of runs we never had any worries about having to defend totals. We were simply trying to bowl sides out all the time. We always had people in catching positions and the lads caught everything. There were some superb catches in every department from Keith Fletcher at slip to Brian Hardie at short leg, and everything went our way.

Our time had come and I think we knew that long before the championship was finally settled. There are certain things that happen as you go through a season which suggest that it is going to be your year, vital moments that change the course of a game when you think you are dead and buried, and we had already experienced that in the Benson and Hedges Cup. It was as though we were meant to win it, as though our name was already on the trophy.

We had lost to Surrey and only just beat Northamptonshire by three runs in the zonal matches and, after beating Warwickshire easily enough in the quarter-final at Chelmsford, we were really up against it against Yorkshire in the semi-final.

We had home advantage again but, after Keith Fletcher had put them in, Yorkshire set off like a train. John Hampshire smashed the ball all round the place and he and Richard Lumb had put on 107 in twenty-nine overs when Hampshire tried to hit Ray East for his second six and was very well caught by Stuart Turner on the midwicket boundary. From 107 without loss just before lunch, Yorkshire collapsed to 173 for nine. And though we made desperately hard work of getting the runs, Neil Smith eventually hit the winning boundary against his native county with three wickets and one over to spare. We had reached our first Lord's final and East and Turner were so emotional about it that they sat down and wept.

At least we did not have too much time to worry about the final itself because we were so involved in the championship. We had a job of work to do and that took our minds off Lord's. It was not until the tickets were allocated and everybody moaned that they had not got enough that we realised that it was going to be a great occasion.

It turned out to be better than that. It was the most wonderful experience of my entire career. The sun shone, Lord's was full and the hairs on the back of my neck stood up when Graham Gooch and Mike Denness went out to open our innings. Seventy-five per cent of the crowd seemed to come from Essex and the roar that greeted them brought me out in goose pimples. I had never heard anything like it from an English crowd. It was more like Eden Gardens, Calcutta, than St John's Wood.

You did not even need to watch the play or look at the scoreboard to know what was happening after that. You knew from the noise of the crowd whether we had hit a four or a six. You knew when we had lost a wicket. And for most of the time it sounded like sweet music to my ears. Keith Fletcher had said beforehand that it was up to the top players to take the pressure off the lesser players and that is exactly what happened as Mike Denness, Ken McEwan and Fletcher played around Gooch, who scored an absolutely majestic 120.

We had scored 290 for six and felt that we could not lose. But we bowled fairly ordinarily and our nerves were beginning to jangle when Geoff Howarth and Roger Knight were putting on ninety-one for the third wicket.

Then came another of those turning points I was talking about. Knight tried to work a ball from Keith Pont on the legside, got an outside edge and Neil Smith dived a long, long way to catch it left handed. It was as crucial as it was spectacular because it eased the pressure again just when they were beginning to claw their way back into the game and put the frighteners on us.

There was one more anxious moment for me – and it was Mike Denness who calmed my fears and convinced me what a splendid influence he was on the side. With Surrey still needing only just over 100 to win with seven wickets and eight overs left, Howarth went for a hook against me and was dropped by Denness himself at fine leg.

A little bit later Mike came wandering across to me and said: "Sorry about that. I should have caught it."

"Don't worry about that," I said. "But what do you think about the way things are going?"

"Och, everything's OK," he replied. "We're well in control. Have no fear about that."

I looked at him and thought to myself: "Well, that'll do for me." He had come across without any embarrassment about dropping the catch, he was not too upset, he was not even too apologetic. And that had a very reassuring effect on me and the other players around who heard him.

Sure enough, we were comfortable winners by thirty-five runs when I bowled Surrey's last man, Hugh Wilson. A jubilant Keith Fletcher threw his arms around me and the celebrations began.

I had arranged for the players, with their wives and girl-friends, to have dinner afterwards, win or lose, at the Victoria Sporting Club, and after the traditional balcony scenes and champagne in the dressing-room we went off to celebrate in style. I still cannot remember how we organised the bill although I think the club might have finished up paying it. But it did not seem to matter at the time. I do recall that it was not a long night because the players were all so exhausted that once they had eaten and had a few beers they just drifted away. The enormity of the occasion had finally got to them.

Not surprisingly, we lost our John Player League match against Yorkshire at Colchester the next day but that did not seem to matter, either. All that concerned us now was the championship and I am sure we would have gone on to win even if another side had got anywhere near us. We were a long way in front, we were playing good cricket and, with the confidence of having our first trophy under our belts, we were ready to go on and complete the job.

With hindsight, we were probably in too much of a hurry because the County Ground at Northampton with the football pitch on one side and the old ramshackled pavilion on the other was not the best place to win the title for the first time in 103 years.

But that was how it worked out. Northamptonshire were going quite well at the time and had reached the final of the Gillette Cup, but Stuart Turner took five wickets in each innings and we were left to get 229 in five hours to win. We got them with ten overs to spare thanks to an unbeaten century from Brian Hardie, but we still had to wait to hear that Worcestershire had failed to win at Derby before we knew that the championship was ours.

The celebrations this time were somewhat muted. There were a few more spectators in the ground than the proverbial three men and a dog, but there could have been no more than forty or fifty staunch Essex supporters present to savour the moment. Some of them had driven up at lunchtime when they learned that we were on the brink of the championship and Peter Edwards, our secretary-manager, had turned up with a few bottles of champagne.

I am not sure that all of them were opened because we had to drive back to Essex, but a few of us were sitting around in the dressing-room having a celebratory drink when the sheer incongruity of the situation was brought home to us. To have a shower in the Northampton pavilion – which I think had been condemned as unfit for human habitation by then – you had to go down to the basement (or cellar, really). And it was from down there that we suddenly heard a tremendous commotion.

"Bang, bang, bang," it went, "whack, whack, whack," until a jubilant voice – I am not sure whether it belonged to Ray East or Keith Pont, but it must have been one or the other – yelled out: "It's OK, you can come down now. I've got 'em!" He claimed that he'd been killing rats.

With respect to Northampton, who have worked so hard to bring their ground up to date in recent years, it was that sort of place and we all had a good laugh before getting into our cars and driving home. It would have been so much nicer to have won it in front of our own supporters and though we did get a much better reception when we played Surrey in our next home match it was not until we walked out for the first match of the following season that they really made us feel like county champions.

They gave us a great send-off that day and it meant an awful lot to us. It did get through to us and make us feel that we had become part of Essex history. There had been many sides and many famous names who had represented the county since it was formed in 1876, but we were the first ones to win the greatest honour. And Fletcher made a great play of that.

It is, after all, the captain's job to make his players believe in themselves because if you believe you are a good side you can do all sorts of things. And it was a lot easier for Fletcher to get us to believe it after we had won something and we went from strength to strength.

I do not know what would have happened, though, if we had not made the breakthrough that season. It would probably have been in one of the limited-overs competitions because they are easier to win. You just need things to go your way on the day. What I do know is that we could not have gone on for ever without winning anything. There would have had to be changes, although Fletcher would undoubtedly have fought against them.

In the meantime I felt that we were popular winners – not just in Essex but throughout the country. It was because we had never won anything before and I think the same feeling would exist if a side like Gloucestershire, who have been so close over the years, were to win the championship for the first time. Everyone, the opposition, their supporters, even the press, seemed genuinely pleased.

As we went on to collect more trophies, you could feel the mood begin to change. People wanted to see some other underdogs coming up and doing well rather than the same side winning all the time. But we could not let that affect our attitude and Fletcher began to push us even harder than he had done before. Pre-season training got tougher, we did our homework on the opposition and we became a highly professional outfit.

At the same time, Essex became highly professional on the administrative side of the club as well. Starting with our success in drawing the crowds on Sundays, we had become a very marketable county and in Peter Edwards we had found just the man to make the most of the situation. It had been a costly business moving the whole circus around the eight grounds we used to use but now Brentwood, Romford, Leyton, Clacton and Westcliff had all gone to allow for the development of the County Ground at Chelmsford. And from that base, Peter Edwards – a chartered secretary with considerable marketing skills who had only joined the club in 1979 –

soon had a prize package to sell: county champions and
Benson and Hedges Cup holders.

5

The Vaseline
Smear

More than two years before Essex won anything at all I
had already won my first England caps – and Robin
Hobbs always insisted that I should have had one a year
before that. He was always pulling your leg about
something or other, but he was adamant that when
Lancashire's Peter Lever was recalled to the England
side for the second Test against Australia at Lord's in
1975 they got the wrong man. According to Hobbs, they
intended to pick John Lever, not Peter.

I do not know how true that is and I have never
bothered to try to find out. At least it meant that I was
beginning to be thought of as an England bowler – even if
it was only by Hobbsy! – and in 1976 I made it my
ambition to be selected for that winter's tour of India, Sri
Lanka and Australia for the Centenary Test match.

The 1975 season had been my best so far with
eighty-two wickets at only twenty runs apiece. And
though I took only sixty-two wickets at twenty-six each in
1976 I had every reason to believe that I was on the fringe
of selection. Tony Greig had taken over the England
captaincy from Mike Denness and I knew that Keith
Fletcher was his right-hand man. And he gave me every

encouragement. "Keep going," he used to say, "and you'll get your chance this winter."

He was right, as he so often is, because I am sure it was my growing reputation for being able to keep going that got me in the squad. Swing bowlers had done reasonably well in India where most of the pitches are not conducive to out-and-out fast bowling so the selectors were obviously looking for somebody who could move the ball in the air. And, no doubt, they thought the fact that I bowled left-arm over would add variety to the attack. But I think it was my fitness record more than anything that attracted them. They probably saw me as someone who could be relied upon to stay fit and come into the side if anybody else got injured, and I set my stall out to convince them that I could fill that role.

I did not think that I was fitter than anybody else, actually; I just thought that I was luckier in that I did not break down as often as other quick bowlers of the time like Bob Willis, Mike Hendrick and Chris Old. And that was probably because I was the right shape for the job. Fred Trueman would doubtless say the same thing about himself, whereas somebody like Willis, superb bowler that he was, was definitely the wrong shape with his gangly, 6ft. 6in. frame and all the working parts liable to strain.

My height was just about right and my action was such that it did not put too much stress on any particular part of my body. I was criticised in my younger days for the length of my run-up, but that was never a problem to me. My legs have always been strong, probably because of all the running I did when I was a schoolboy. I never bothered with a bicycle but just used to run to school or to cricket or to football so the criticism about running too far to bowl did not worry me because I knew it was not taking anything out of me. If it had detracted from my bowling then I might have listened, but that long run-up actually helped my bowling. It helped my rhythm and the fact that I also had to walk back a long way helped me to recover.

At that stage I had only had one serious injury problem, apart from minor pulls and strains, and that was a pinched muscle under the ribs – a common fast bowler's complaint. I carried the injury for a few games because I thought I could get through it and then kept trying to come back too soon. In the end I had to take a good three-week rest which cleared it up and, by 1976, I had proved that I could bowl thirty overs in a day without too much stress.

It is one thing, of course, to be considered for England selection and another actually to get on to the plane and many of us have had our disappointments over the years. You can be so near to getting on it throughout the summer and yet so far away when it actually takes off. When I got home one night and my parents told me that they had heard on the radio that I was in the squad of sixteen I was so elated that it is difficult now to describe my feelings.

Suddenly it was just like Christmas. I went up to Lord's and was given all the gear that is handed out to touring cricketers – plus an armful of injections that was not quite as pleasant. And when I went to Burton's to be measured for my tour blazer I felt a million dollars, I really did. There was a party, too, thrown by the people at Ilford, who invited my parents as well as all my friends and gave me an enormous card with a sketch of me on an elephant to wish me good luck in India.

The tour itself could not have started better from my point of view. We were using Indian balls which swung all over the place, and after taking thirteen wickets in my first three games I felt that I was bowling as well as anybody in the party. With Bob Willis and Chris Old sure to open the attack, the third bowling place had always seemed to be between Mike Selvey and myself and I was quietly confident of being picked for the first Test in Delhi. The side is not named until the team dinner the night before, but you get some idea from the previous game because they usually play the probable Test side – and I had match figures of 7 for 59 in that. Meanwhile Keith Fletcher was dropping all sorts of hints and, sure enough, when the team was finally announced I was in it.

I was still on tenterhooks, though, because no sooner had Tony Greig revealed the team than he was telling the players who had been left out: "Don't forget, boys. Remember we are in India and it will only take one bout of diarrhoea [or words to that effect!] and you'll be in."

Then Bernard Thomas, our physiotherapist, came up and said: "Do you want anything to help you sleep? It won't be easy, you know."

"No thanks, Bernard," I said. "I'll be all right." And I did get off to sleep reasonably well. It was what happened afterwards that was to cause me countless sleepless nights.

Next morning Greig won the toss but we made a disastrous start, losing our first four wickets for sixty-five before Greig himself and Alan Knott, batting as artfully as only he could, helped Dennis Amiss to pull the innings round. Despite a chest complaint, Amiss went on to bat for eight and a half hours, scoring 179, and I joined him in an eighth-wicket stand of ninety-four. Having gone in as night watchman, I finished up with fifty-three, which was to be my highest score in thirty-one Test innings, and England with 381.

Yet if that was a sensational enough start to my Test career, it was nothing compared with what came next. We had had a choice of three different makes of Indian balls and we had picked the brand that had swung around in the earlier games. Although the one we used at the start of the Indian innings did not seem to do too much for Willis and Old, it quickly went out of shape and we had it changed after eleven overs.

And as soon as I came on for my first bowl in Test cricket the replacement ball really did swing. In the space of sixteen deliveries I took four wickets – those of Anshuman Gaekwad, Mohinder Amarnath, Gundappa Viswanath and Venkataraghavan. And after Gavaskar and Patel had threatened a recovery next morning I dismissed both of them and also picked up Kirmani before India were all out for 122.

I had taken seven for forty-six on my Test debut but it did not sink in for a moment. Having got four of my wickets the night before, it just did not register that I had taken seven in the innings – until Keith Fletcher came racing towards me from second slip with a grin from ear to ear.

"What's the matter with you?" I said, puzzled by the look on his face which was one of such joy and happiness that I will never forget it as long as I live.

"I'm just happy for you," he said.

I got three more wickets when India followed on to give me match figures of 10 for 70 and despite a long delay because of fog India only just managed to take the match into the fifth day before losing by an innings and twenty-five runs.

The reaction was incredible. Telegrams flooded in, not just from relatives and friends in Ilford where I had played all my cricket, not only from all over Essex and other counties in England, but from all parts of India as well. It could not have been easy for them after losing a Test match so comprehensively. It could not have been easy for some of them to put their words into English. But there they were, pencilled out on the telegrams: "Super"; "Well done"; "Lovely bowling"; "Great performance". I kept them all.

Suddenly I was a national hero and the BBC wanted to

interview me and Tony Greig. We could not keep the team bus waiting so the rest of the players returned to the hotel with Greigy saying: "Don't worry, we'll get back OK." And as soon as we had completed the interviews he went outside and stopped two motor scooters. He got on the back of one of them, told me to get on the back of the other and away we went.

It was rush hour in Delhi. In fact it always seemed to be rush hour in Delhi. There were buses, trucks, cars, motor-cycles, motorised rickshaws, bullock carts, every means of transport you can imagine, and there we were dodging in and out of it on the pillions of these two tiny scooters.

"This is it," I thought to myself. "I've just got into the England side and I'm going to get knocked off this thing and crushed to death."

The scooter-rider did not do much to reassure me, either. He could not seem to comprehend that he had got Tony Greig, captain of England, in front of him and John Lever, the guy who had just taken all these wickets in the Test, behind, and he kept turning round to have a look at me. "I'm still here," I yelled above the roar of the traffic. "Keep your eyes on the road."

For me, it was like something out of *Boy's Own* and, once we had reached the sanctuary of our hotel, I could not have been happier. Indeed it was turning out to be a very happy tour all round and our spirits soared even higher when we went to Calcutta for the second Test and won that one as well, depite all kinds of problems through injury and illness.

Keith Fletcher had badly damaged his ankle tripping over a step the night before the match, which happened to be New Year's Eve although it was not through too much drink. He was far too professional for that. Derek Underwood was so ill overnight that he was a doubtful starter until just before we left the hotel and Tony Greig was running a high temperature. Yet with Greig scoring a selfless century and reserve wicketkeeper Roger Tolchard, playing as a batsman, and Derek Randall, making his debut, also getting runs we won easily by ten wickets.

Then came the incident that was to take the gloss off everything that had gone before and turn me from a hero to a villain overnight. The third Test was being played at Madras, which is hotter and stickier than anywhere else that Test cricket is staged in India. Sweat stings when it runs into your eyes, so I asked Bernard Thomas for some Vaseline to smear across the top of my eyebrows to channel it down the side of my face in the same way as boxers and, occasionally, footballers do to keep the sweat out of their eyes. Dear old Bernard did not have any Vaseline and came up with what he thought was the next best thing – Vaseline impregnated gauze.

We did not think any more about it for the first two days of the Test as we batted first and scored 262 and then began to make considerable inroads into the Indian batting. It was not until after lunch on the third day – by which time the Indian first innings was almost over – that Bob Willis and I decided to try using strips of the gauze to keep the sweat out of our eyes. It simply did not work and after a short time I ripped mine off and threw it on to the ground close to the stumps. Umpire Reuben immediately snatched it up, apparently, I discovered later, because he considered it to be a breach of Law 46 or, more specifically, Experimental Law 46 Note 4 (iii) which states: "No interference with the natural condition of the ball shall be allowed." And India's captain, Bishen Bedi led the charge that I had been using Vaseline to help me to make the ball swing.

"We've caught him cheating," he told the press. "We've got the proof and we're going to send the ball away for forensic examination."

I did not have a clue what was going on but one or two

of the Indians said to me: "Don't worry about it. He's a Sikh from the north, we're playing in the south and he knows that the selectors are looking to get rid of him. It's his way of fighting back."

Only I did worry. And I worried even more when I arrived at the ground the next morning to be greeted by a huge banner saying: "CHEATER LEVER GO HOME."

There were other messages as well, some of them humorous, like the one advertising a different brand of Vaseline, but others more threatening, and all kinds of wild accusations in the Indian newspapers. And though the Test and County Cricket Board at Lord's quickly accepted the explanation received from Greig and our manager, Ken Barrington, I really did feel like going home at the time.

I had been accused of having to rely on something other than my own ability to get wickets – ten in Delhi, two in Calcutta and seven more in Madras. Yet Bernard had only bought the gauze two days before the third Test so there was no way that it could have been used in the first two. And we had only experimented with it in Madras because it was so hot. It had been so cool in Delhi that I remember wearing a long-sleeved sweater.

What helped enormously was that the English cricket-writers supported me all the way through. I am not sure that the same thing would happen today but, from the cuttings which were sent out, I knew that every single one of them had been kind and understanding and I really did appreciate it. If they had been against me, it would have been unbearable.

What did not help at all, though, was that I had a couple of letters from home telling me that some news reporters were sitting on my parents' doorstep and pestering them about it. And the fact that they were being dragged into the scurrilous accusations that their son was a cheat really did turn me against the man who had made them. After all, Bishen Bedi and I had played against each other in county cricket for years and the only reason he could possibly have had for insinuating that I was the kind of cricketer who would suddenly start cheating in the middle of a Test match was because India were already 2-0 down in the series and about to go 3-0 down – which they duly did when we won that Madras Test by 200 runs.

Apart from anything else, that incident soured the entire series. That was so sad because until then we had got on really well with all the Indian players from batsmen like little Gundappa Viswanath and Dilip Vengsarkar to wicketkeeper Syed Kirmani and spinners Bagwat Chandrasekhar and Eripali Prasanna. They were a great bunch of blokes. But from then on we stopped going into their changing-room and kept our distance.

The mood of the cricket changed as well. We had become the first touring side ever to win the first three Tests of a series in India – and how the Indians made us pay for it! We lost by 140 runs in the fourth Test in Bangalore where Yajuvendra Singh, making his debut, equalled the world record by taking seven catches at short leg – although we felt that umpire Ghouse, who also seemed to have been chosen specifically for that match, should have been given the credit for a few of them.

My mind went back to Delhi and the three LBW decisions I had got in India's first innings – not because I did not think they were out but because of something that Keith Fletcher had said. "Apart from anything else," he had told me, "getting three LBWs was quite incredible in itself." Now I realised what he meant.

We might also have lost the final Test in Bombay – where Sunil Gavaskar had to be warned by the umpires after taking the new ball and running straight down the

middle of what was already a worn and turning pitch –
had not Keith Fletcher made his own distinctive contribution by defying his still troublesome ankle to prove
what a great player of spin bowling he was with a
masterly, match-saving fifty-eight not out.

That meant that we had won the series 3-1 yet it took
the older players – people like Greig, Fletcher, Amiss,
Underwood and Knott, who had played a lot of cricket
out there – to put our achievement into proper perspective for me. They were really chuffed – there is no other
word – by what we had done, but it was only when I went
back there in 1981–82 that I found out for myself how
hard it is even to draw a series in India let alone win one,
especially after going 1-0 down in the first Test!

In retrospect, it was a huge success because India did
not have a bad side at all with batsmen of the quality of
Gavaskar, Viswanath and Vengsarkar, a wicketkeeper
who could bat in Kirmani and the four great spinners,
Chandrasekhar, who was the best I ever saw, Bedi,
Prasanna and Venkataraghavan. Yet we had beaten
them fair and square with our own Derek Underwood
taking more wickets than any of them – twenty-nine – and
me not far behind with twenty-six. And to those of us on
our first tour, it had all seemed fairly straightforward
from a cricketing point of view. We new boys just took it
in our stride and thought: "Right, we've done that job.
Where do we go next? Oh, yes. Australia for the
Centenary Test. That's just a friendly game, isn't it?"

Quite honestly, I went to Australia with that in mind
and it was only when we arrived in Melbourne – via
Colombo and Perth where we drew with Sri Lanka and
Western Australia in totally contrasting conditions – that
I realised how wrong we were. It was the festival of
Moomba, an Aboriginal word meaning "Let's get
together and have fun", in Melbourne and every living
cricketer who had ever played for England or Australia

seemed to be doing just that. Looking back now, I only wish I could have enjoyed it a little bit more myself.

We had been on tour for almost four months – the longest time I had ever been away from home. Although I overcame my initial homesickness through the companionship of players like Geoff Miller and Bob Willis, I did find it a bit hard to take when instead of getting on a plane to go home after trekking all round India and Sri Lanka we flew just as far the other way. With the possible exception of Derek Randall, we would all have savoured the Centenary Test more if we had not been so exhausted by all the hard work we had put in beforehand – and if we had been better prepared for what was in store.

As it was, we played a warm-up game against Western Australia in Perth, which was not very good practice for playing in Melbourne because the pitches were completely different – Perth bounced a lot, Melbourne did not bounce at all – and then discovered that the occasion was not quite what we had envisaged. The organisation was fantastic, the crowds were huge, averaging between 60,000 and 70,000 a day, and, far from treating it as a friendly game, the Aussies were dying to win it. Dennis Lillee had been making a few war-like noises when we had arrived in Perth but we had not realised that he was deadly serious until we saw Rick McCosker coming back in to bat with his head swathed in bandages after having his jaw broken by Bob Willis.

It turned out to be an unforgettable game of cricket – and I had the honour of bowling the first ball to Australia's opening batsman Ian Davis. I took his wicket as well but after we had bowled them out for 138 they bowled us out for 95. Then the battle was really joined. David Hookes, hitting Greig for five fours in one over, and Doug Walters thrilled the crowd with their stroke-play and Rod Marsh hit an unbeaten hundred to set us 463 to win. Mike Brearley, Dennis Amiss, Tony Greig, and Alan Knott all made runs but it was Derek Randall who really captured the public imagination with an unbelievable 174.

In the end we lost by just forty-five runs – by an amazing coincidence the same result as the first Test a hundred years earlier. It had been a great game to play in but we were all a little disappointed that we had actually lost. We felt that with Derek Randall playing the way he did we should have won it. After all, forty-five runs are not that many when you are chasing a target of 463.

So ended my first England tour. I am sure it helped me to mature as a player and I like to think that I took some of that maturity back to Essex. But it also left me with a touch of bitterness that, I am sorry to say, lasts to this day.

The day after I got home, I flew off again to play in a double-wicket tournament in South Africa. It was only when I got back from there that I was met at the airport by David Tack, my oldest and closest friend, who had to break the news to me that my father had suffered a heart attack.

I knew that dad had recently started a driving job which was not agreeing with him particularly well, but I could not help thinking that the stress and the strain brought about by all those headlines about his son being charged with cheating in his very first Test series had not done him any good at all. That made me feel very bitter indeed towards the chap I held responsible for having all that rubbish splashed across the newspapers.

That bitterness was to spill over into the next English season when my first sight of Bishen Bedi playing for Northamptonshire caused all sorts of problems – not for me, because I was bowling the bouncers, but for him, because he was on the receiving end. I made it perfectly clear that I did not like him and that whatever he said would not put things right.

He was not a bad guy at all, really. In fact he was well thought of wherever he played and I had always regarded him as a friend. The following year he came across to me wanting to shake hands and bury the hatchet, as it were.

By then, I suppose, I should have been prepared to forgive and forget, but I still could not bring myself to do it. I may have been making too much of it, but the thought that my father might have had his heart attack as a result of all the strife and aggravation he caused was, to me, unforgivable.

6

The Great Motivator

I went on three more England tours but none of them was quite as magical as that first trip under Tony Greig. Despite our defeat in the Centenary Test, it was a triumphant campaign and we were all proud to be part of his team.

What we did not know was that even before that momentous match in Melbourne some of the top Australian players had already signed contracts to play for Kerry Packer, the owner of a television channel, and most of the others were to do so during it. Although he has since denied that he had any knowledge of Packer's plans while he was captaining England, it was not long before Greig was virtually acting as his recruiting agent in other parts of the world.

Among those who signed were four members of that touring party – Dennis Amiss and the Kent trio of Alan Knott, Derek Underwood and Bob Woolmer, which was hardly surprising since they would not blow their noses without consulting one another about it.

I honestly knew nothing about what was going on myself and nor would I have expected to. Knowing Greig as well as I did by then, he was not going to approach somebody like me who had only just played in his first Test series to join an organisation that was going to split world cricket and obviously be at loggerheads with the Test and County Cricket Board. But I am sure he felt – and rightly so – that even if I had been approached I would have said no.

I was very much against the whole thing anyway. At the time I was on the committee of the Cricketers' Association and, having just started my own Test career, I was protective towards Test cricket – not just for its sake or my own sake but for the good of county cricketers in general. I thought that if this chap Packer was going to sign up all the best players and make a mess of Test series all round the world, it would have an adverse effect on everybody. And I was heavily involved in the debate.

In fact I actually went to meet Packer with Jack Bannister, the secretary of the Cricketers' Association, and various other people at a London hotel where he put his case to us. I was sure it went a lot deeper but, basically, he was trying to wrestle the rights for televising cricket in Australia away from the Australian Broadcasting Commission. And it was very easy to see why somebody like Greig, who was always keenly interested in the commercial side of things, took to him so instantly. Packer was as big and brash as his cartoon image, but he was also as persuasive as he was forthright and listening to him that day you could understand how he could make people believe that he was right and everybody else was wrong.

Looking back now, I suppose he got just about everything he wanted – and I have to admit that the way that he did it was far better than most of us expected. From growing pitches in hot-houses and placing them in the middle of football grounds to playing night cricket under floodlights, from using white balls and kitting the players out in coloured clothing to introducing circles to discourage defensive field-placings, his innovations were highly successful. And, according to the players I spoke to, the cricket itself was quite good and certainly fiercely contested.

A lot of benefits flowed from World Series Cricket, too, most significantly the upgrading of Test status for England players. Test cricketers in Australia, India and Pakistan had always been well thought of and comparatively well rewarded as professional sportsmen, but it was not like that in England until Packer came on the scene and kicked the Test and County Cricket Board into the twentieth century.

Cornhill's sponsorship enabled the TCCB to give the England players huge pay rises and, although the Packer revolution has not done anything like as much for the ordinary county cricketer as Greig predicted it would – they had to wait a little bit longer for their pay increases and many are probably still waiting! – it has improved the financial situation for most of the county clubs, which are now making money instead of just about breaking even. Packer showed them how to promote and market the game and that has not done us any harm. We probably play too much one-day cricket but it provides a lot of fun and, as Peter Edwards of Essex says, his biggest selling-point in these days of changing values is that we still have the game of cricket we have always known and loved.

In fact, if World Series Cricket was ever going to cause real damage to the established game it would have been in its first season (1977–78) when Packer suddenly released three of his Pakistani players – Mushtaq Mohammad, Zaheer Abbas and Imran Khan – to play against us in the final Test in Karachi. We were so opposed to their inclusion that there was a very real threat of the England team going on strike. We spoke on the telephone to Doug Insole, then chairman of the Test and County Cricket Board, and Donald Carr, the secretary, and they made it clear that the game had to go on. I think Doug sympathised with our feelings but he was looking for what was best for international cricket as a whole. I dare say that he might have been able to talk us out of it, but a strike was still a distinct possibility until the eve of the Test when the Pakistan Board belatedly made it clear that the Packer men would not be chosen.

We did not know it at the time but, from talking to them afterwards, we discovered that the senior Pakistanis who had played in the first two Tests – people like Wasim Bari, the captain, Wasim Raja, Sarfraz Nawaz and Javed Miandad – were strongly in favour of our action and so, with both sets of players opposed to the idea of them playing, the "Packerstanis", as *Wisden* dubbed them, turned round and went back to Australia.

With that crisis averted, I suppose the worst aspect of the whole affair from my point of view was that England lost Tony Greig. I was very sad about that because I had got on very well with him. I had only just got into the England team and was still a little bit shy with some of the senior players who I did not know so well. But I never felt shy with Greigy. You could not help but like him and it was very easy to become a Greig man and feel that you were one of his team.

Actually Greig was not the first England captain I played under. I had been on a couple of tours to South Africa with Derrick Robins' teams and, on the second of them, Brian Close was our skipper. Ray East was in that side, too, but it did not take him long to discover that he was not going to be playing a lot of cricket. We were chatting about who would bowl spin in support of the Australian, John Gleeson, who was also with us, when Closey said: "When my fingers are loose, I can bowl a few spinners." And so he did, most memorably against

Hylton Ackerman, a formidable hitter who kept smashing the ball all over Cape Town.

But it was when we were rained off one day in one of the earlier matches that we discovered just how much of an all-rounder Close considered himself to be. We had heard that he had been a professional footballer, we knew that he was a considerable golfer either left-handed or right, but we were still not prepared for what was coming as we listened on the radio to news of Muhammad Ali's latest title defence. His opponent had been paid something like a million pounds for the privilege of being beaten by the greatest heavyweight boxer of all time, and Closey said: "I would get in the ring for that. I could do it. He might hit me but he wouldn't hurt me."

We looked at one another quizzically, thinking: "Blimey, this bloke's going to be our captain for the next six weeks," before going off to a local gym to do a bit of circuit training. And it was as Ray East and I were putting in a few laps that we glanced into the middle of the gym and saw Closey . . . shadow boxing!

I really do believe that he had meant what he said. He would have got into the ring with Ali and, while "The Greatest" might well have hit him a few times, I am sure he would not have hurt him.

Now I am not saying that Tony Greig would ever have contemplated getting into the ring with Muhammad Ali, but he did have the same kind of belief in himself as Close did. What made him such a great motivator was that he could pass that belief on to his players so that they started to believe in themselves as well.

As a player, he always had his critics but if you look at his record (58 Tests; 3,599 runs at 40.43; 141 wickets at 32.20) it compares very favourably with that of Trevor Bailey (61 Tests; 2,290 runs at 29.74; 132 wickets at 29.21), and Trevor is always considered to have been one of England's finest all-rounders.

As a batsman, Greig loved to take the fight to the bowlers when England had their backs to the wall, as he did in Australia in 1974–75 when everyone else was being peppered by Lillee and Thomson and he was crashing them to the pickets and then signalling the boundaries himself. As a bowler, he reminded me of Doug Walters when he was known as the "golden arm" of the Australian side. "Give it to Dougie," they would say, "and he'll get us a wicket." It was much the same with Greig. Everybody would be scratching their heads when he came on and thinking, "Why isn't Bob Willis bowling?" and suddenly he would strangle a wicket somewhere.

But that was not all England lost when Greig defected to Packer. Ironically, in view of what happened, they also lost a leader who made you believe that there was no greater honour than playing for your country, that you were head and shoulders above whoever you were playing against and that nothing was impossible. And if you won, you had achieved the ultimate. You could not do any more than that and for one night at least the world was yours.

Tactically, he relied heavily on Keith Fletcher, but that did not count against him as far as I was concerned. He could do his side of the job very well and if he wanted advice about anything else he was never too big or too proud to seek it from someone who had a better cricketing brain. And he did have ideas of his own.

One of them was that in the nets everybody had to have batting practice. He would not just let the batsmen bat and the bowlers bowl. We all had to get in there – and we knew that if Greig himself bowled at us he would probably let us have a bouncer or two. I have been on some tours where I never even put on a pair of pads in the nets, which was my own fault entirely, of course, but I never had a choice under Greig. And I honestly believe that it was because I had nets all the way through that I got so many runs on that tour.

In fact I scored 122, which was rather more than some of the unfortunate England batsmen like Keith Fletcher, Derek Randall, Bob Woolmer and Graham Barlow, but considerably fewer than Mike Brearley, which may surprise many people. They tend to forget that when he took over the England captaincy from Greig he was already in the side as a batsman and was not just chosen, initially at any rate, for his qualities of leadership.

These were nothing like Greig's. Brearley got the best out of people in a completely different way ... with a quiet word here and there rather than the "Up and at 'em for England and the Union Jack!" approach. Brearley was a little more subtle than that and nothing illustrated his approach better than the contrasting ways in which he coaxed so many match-winning performances out of Ian Botham and Bob Willis.

Some people will always say that Brearley was lucky to have Botham in his side at a time when the most prodigious all-round cricketer the game has ever known was completing the double of 1,000 runs and 100 wickets in his first twenty-one Tests. What they do not recognise – and what the England selectors failed to recognise at the time – was that Botham needed Brearley just as much as Brearley needed Botham.

Brearley realised at a very early stage in Botham's Test career that for all his massive talent and boundless self-confidence, the youngster desperately needed someone to believe in him. And Brearley showed Botham that he did believe in him by giving him his head and never trying to restrain his natural attacking instincts.

It was in Botham's character never to be daunted by a temporary setback. If he bowled a bouncer and got hooked for four or six, then nine times out of ten the ball that followed was another bouncer, only this time shorter, higher and infinitely quicker as if to say: "You've done it to me once but you won't do it again."

Sometimes, of course, he paid the price – like he did in the second Test against Australia at Perth on the 1978–79 tour. Peter Toohey was one of the new batsmen who had come into the Australian side following the defection of the Packer men and "Both" decided to give him the bouncer treatment. He bounced him three or four times in one over and Toohey kept smacking him for four. But one boundary only just scraped over midwicket's head and that was all the encouragement "Both" needed to keep up the barrage.

It was not good bowling on a pitch that was not all that quick against one of the better hookers in the Australian side who finally ran out of partners on eighty-one – his highest score against England. But that was Botham's way ... and Brearley skilfully channelled all that natural aggression in the right direction with quite sensational results.

With Bob Willis it was different. Apart from responding to the normal encouragement from his captain, Botham could also be provoked into dynamic action by such taunts as: "You're bowling like an old tart." But that sort of thing did not work at all with Bob. He had such an inferiority complex about his bowling that he would try anything, including hypnotic tapes, to overcome it so it was evident that he needed to be reassured about the quality of his bowling rather than roused to greater effort. And Brearley would do it superbly with words like, "You're a better bowler than he is a batsman," or, "I don't know how you keep going, I really don't."

Just how much both Willis and Botham needed Brearley's support and guidance was there for all to see in 1980 when Botham was given the awful burden of captaining England in successive series against the West Indies – apparently on the recommendation of Brearley, who was reluctant to go on any more tours. Suddenly he had lost his mentor and with no one else in the side to take over that role he went through the worst patch of his career. At the same time, Botham could not get the best out of Willis, either, and it was only when the selectors reverted to Brearley during the summer of 1981 that they both made an almost miraculous return to form in that unforgettable victory over Australia at Headingley.

It was never going to be easy for somebody doing all the jobs that Botham was doing – bowling long spells, batting at number six (invariably under pressure), catching everything in the slips – to take on the captaincy as well, especially against a side as powerful as the West Indies had then become. But I have often wondered what might have happened if the selectors had stayed with him for just a little bit longer.

Since then, I have realised how much the cares of captaincy can affect a class player by witnessing what happened to Graham Gooch when he first took over from Keith Fletcher at Essex. And I have also seen what can happen when such players are given time to grow into the job.

Australia, as is their way, appointed Allan Border for much the same reason as England appointed Botham – because he was their best player and, therefore, the one most likely to keep his place in the side – and although he was never a natural leader they stuck with him until he had learned the art of captaincy.

Who is to say that if the England selectors had stuck with Botham he would not have come good and developed into a really successful England captain? It is something that we will always argue about.

In the meantime, we did know that Geoff Boycott was not the right man for the job. He had taken over for the final Test in Pakistan and all three Tests in New Zealand on that 1977–78 tour after Mike Brearley had broken his arm in a practice match and returned home – and that was enough to convince us that he could never be a good captain because of the narrow, self-centred view he had of his own game.

That attitude manifested itself most vividly in the second Test against New Zealand at Christchurch, which happened to be the only one he actually won. We had lost the first Test in Wellington on a brute of a pitch, Richard Hadlee taking ten wickets in the match to give New Zealand their first victory over England in forty-eight years and forty-eight Tests. The second Test was memorable enough for the fact that it was really the launch of Botham's spectacular career as he scored a century and then took five wickets in the first innings. But it was on the fourth afternoon that the real drama began to unfold.

We had to score some quick runs if we were going to give ourselves a chance of bowling them out on the last day but Boycott seemed oblivious to the situation until Willis, by then the vice-captain, decided to take a hand. He sent Botham in to speed things up – which he did by running out his captain by the length of the pitch. That upset Boycott so much that on his return to the changing-room he sat with a towel over his head while the game took its course without him seeming to take the slightest interest in what was happening.

It was Bob Willis who kept things going the next morning when he suggested that, with a lead of 279, we had enough runs to declare. Everybody else agreed with him – apart from Boycott who seemed to be the only one looking on the negative side and arguing against it. In the end he did declare, Bob bowled as fast as he has ever done, we levelled the series and "Boycs" was once again back to his happy, jovial self.

Once that story got around, his chances of ever captaining England on a long-term basis had virtually disappeared – and in some ways that was a pity. He was never a problem as far as I was concerned. In fact I got on very well with him, especially in the nets where I thought that he was great value. He was always trying to get the best out of you, giggling if he hit you for four and provoking you into trying that much harder.

"Let's try and hit 'Boycs' on the inside of the thigh," was the attitude of the bowlers – or, in Botham's case, "Let's try and hit 'Boycs' on the head!"

Yet he relished the challenge because it ensured that he himself would have a better net. That was totally selfish, of course, but it did make you bowl better yourself and, from that point of view, I think that we all benefited from it.

You could learn a great deal simply from talking to Boycott, too. He was very interesting when you could get him to talk as a batsman about the bowlers he had to face, and he was absolutely brilliant at putting himself in the position of the bowler and discussing how he would bowl at various batsmen. He taught me about this kind of role-reversal, making me think as a batsman, working out what he would expect from the bowler and how he would be planning to play it. And I often thought how much more we could have got out of him had he done more of that, especially with the younger players. But, then, so could Yorkshire.

The problem with Boycott was that he would not always come out with it. It often seemed to be too much for him to worry about other people's games when he was worrying so much about his own. And that was a great shame because there was so much knowledge there just waiting to be tapped.

So, when Brearley finally decided to call it a day, the selectors turned instead to Keith Fletcher – and I have never been able to understand why he was discarded after just that one tour of India and Sri Lanka in 1981–82.

I have tried to think of every possible reason why he

should have got the sack when he got home – that the whole trip was fairly negative with not much good cricket coming out of it after we had lost the first Test and consequently the series 1-0; that his slight misdemeanour (so trivial that I had almost forgotten it) when he showed his utter frustration by flicking off a bail must have caused deep offence to new chairman Peter May; or that they somehow felt that he must have had something to do with so many of us signing secret deals to play in South Africa, which he certainly knew nothing about.

But in the end I had to come to the conclusion that he had never been looked on as anything other than a stop-gap captain because there is no other way I can equate what happened to him with what should happen in the game of cricket. It seems to me that they must already have made up their minds that they were not going to retain him for the first Test against India the following summer because if they had, and had he made runs, they would have been stuck with him.

It all seemed very strange to me. I did not think that Fletcher did a bad job at all in India when you consider the problems that he had to cope with – not least the extraordinary behaviour of that man Boycott, who seemed to lose all interest after breaking Sir Garfield Sobers' record of 8,032 runs on his way to a century in the third Test at Delhi.

The tour management had already had difficulties with him over various matters, including his habit of going to see the hotel chefs to get them to make up special meals for him. Indian cuisine has never worried me because I like curry anyway, but it is not to everyone's taste and I have seen people like Graham Roope going through a whole tour on eggs and Alan Knott apparently living on nothing but fried bananas. The trouble with Boycott's fads was that we were signing for our meals and his bills were three or four times bigger than anyone else's.

His supporters will no doubt say that he was three or four times better than some of the rest of us, but that was just one of the problems that had to be sorted out. The final straw that persuaded the management not to make any more allowances for his idiosyncracies came during the fourth Test at Calcutta when he said he was too sick to go to the ground. I remember it well because I had been made twelfth man and I was fielding for him when it was discovered that he was not at the hotel, where we had left him, but out on the golf course. His explanation was that Bernard Thomas had told him to try to get a bit of fresh air – which is not that easy in Calcutta, I must admit – and he thought that was the best way to do it, but most of the players felt it was a pretty lame excuse.

It was not easy for Fletcher and the manager, Raman Subba Row, to take the decision to send him home because, quite honestly, some of us thought that that was what he wanted anyway. But Fletcher did not feel that you could have a successful or a happy touring side with one member of it just doing his own thing.

I do not know if any other England captain has ever had such a tough decision to make – but I did feel that Fletcher, having made it, did deserve at least to be given the chance that every previous captain had been given – which was to lead England in England. Just to have taken the side out once at home would have been the pinnacle of his career and I think he could have come to terms with it if the selectors had said to him: "Look, you're thirty-eight now so we'd just like you to do the first Test match and then we'll be looking for another skipper to take over."

As it was, he could not come to terms with what they did to him and, as a result, Essex drifted through that summer without his usual sharp leadership – for which he apologised at the start of the following season.

Fletcher's successor was Bob Willis and I was not surprised that he found the job very difficult. No one has more respect for Bob than I do because, although I never played under him, I had seen what he could do, not just in that Christchurch Test but also in Colombo where he really let rip when we were not exactly covering ourselves in glory in Sri Lanka's inaugural Test, and roused us from our lethargy to win comfortably enough in the end.

But I am not speaking with hindsight when I say that I, in common with a lot of other cricketers, always felt that he would find it hard for the simple reason that any bowler, but especially an opening bowler, would find it hard. And for somebody like Bob, who invariably gave more than 110 per cent and almost seemed to go into a trance when he was bowling, it was virtually impossible to take a step back and assess the game.

I did not play under David Gower, either, but just as I felt that Bob was too intense for the job so I suspected that David would be too laid-back to be acceptable to everybody. But he did recover from his baptism of fire against the West Indies to achieve the considerable feat of beating India in India and Australia at home before coming the inevitable cropper against the West Indies again. Then the selectors dismissed him for what many of us felt was the silliest of reasons ... because they wanted someone to take a higher profile and be more noticeable on the field.

That could mean only one man – the hand-clapping, ear-splitting Mike Gatting. And, having informed Gower of their decision in the worst possible way (i.e. *after* his successor had been appointed) they really did seem to be giving Gatting a decent run in the job when they dismissed him as well in what seemed to be even more bizarre circumstances, apparently accepting his explanation for some scandalous headlines in a tabloid newspaper but still sacking him anyway.

To be fair to the selectors, that was only the catalyst since he was already in trouble for breaking his contract for the ill-fated Pakistan tour by writing a book on the subject and allowing parts of it to be published in a Sunday newspaper – and he had led England in fifteen Tests without a victory. But I was still not too impressed by their man-management which resulted in England having four captains in one series – Gatting, John Emburey, Chris Cowdrey and Graham Gooch. And I have to say that, like Botham, Willis, Gower and Fletcher before them, none of the four had long enough in the job for anyone to make a proper judgement on them.

They are all close friends of mine and I found it quite distressing to see them all given the England captaincy and then have it taken away from them.

I felt most sorry for Fletcher because I actually saw the effect that it had on him . . . but I thought that what they did to every single one of them was pretty dreadful.

7

A Rebel in
South Africa

When Mike Brearley stood up at a meeting of the
Cricketers' Association to discuss the ramifications of the
so-called rebel tour to South Africa in 1982, he said that
those of us who took part in it had done exactly the same
as the players who had gone to play for Kerry Packer
more than four years earlier. However, I felt that it was
totally different.

Looking back now, I can understand why people like
Brearley felt that way. They thought that we were putting
Test cricket in jeopardy just as I had believed the Packer
men were, but, at the time, I did not think that we were
doing that at all. I just thought that we were putting our
own Test careers in some jeopardy, and although there
were some cutting remarks from the floor of the meeting I
did not take too much notice of them. Funnily enough,
they came from people who, I am sure, would have gone
to South Africa themselves if they had been asked.

To put my feelings into perspective, I should point out
that I knew nothing about the South African project until
just a few days before the end of the England tour of India
and Sri Lanka. I had played in only two of the seven Tests
and, though I had taken a few wickets, I had not had a

very happy time. In fact, I was convinced that my Test career was over. So when a meeting was called in Colombo – by Bob Willis, I seem to remember – to put the South African offer to some of us, I was more than interested.

My situation was simple. I had played in twenty Test matches – fifteen of them on four overseas tours – but after my initial success in India I had never really commanded a regular place in the England side. My position had started to change as early as the 1977–78 trip to Pakistan and New Zealand when Ian Botham first came to the fore and I had to compete for the other seam bowling places with Bob Willis, Chris Old and Mike Hendrick. It was towards the end of that tour that I started carrying the drinks tray and I must have finished up by being twelfth man in as many Test matches as I actually played.

It was in that role, incidentally, that I committed the most unprofessional act of my cricket life. It happened at Nottingham in 1981 where all the talk around the dinner-table on the eve of the Test convinced me that I would not be in the final eleven, so I went out and had a few drinks . . . and a few more drinks. Next morning, my alarm call did not materalise for some reason, all the team's attempts to contact me failed as well and it was 10.30 by the time I woke up.

It was quite the worst feeling I have ever known and I still have nightmares about throwing on my tie and blazer, jumping into the car and driving out of the Albany Hotel into a solid mass of traffic. Everybody else in Nottingham seemed to be trying to get to the Test match as well and I just had to sit there for what felt like hours. When I eventually got to Trent Bridge, with the first ball about to be bowled, the gateman would not let me in and he was on the car bonnet calling for a policeman as I raced up the pavilion steps and into the changing-room.

There, with Bob Willis and one or two more sniggering behind my back, I had to apologise to Mike Brearley and Alec Bedser, then chairman of the selectors, explaining lamely: "I didn't think I was going to play."

Brearley pointed out, quite rightly, that if somebody like Willis or Mike Hendrick had twisted an ankle in the nets that morning I would have had to play and there was no arguing with that. I had let myself down and I knew it.

But that was a sheer lack of professionalism and nothing really to do with the fact that I had been made twelfth man. I never resented that at all because I was only too pleased to be involved.

I must admit, though, that there were times when I sat there with very itchy feet just wishing I could have been out there playing – and never more so than in New Zealand. With Hendrick and Botham both laid low by amoebic dysentery and unable to take any part, I had played in all three Tests in Pakistan on the 1977–78 tour – all of them on flat pitches and all of them drawn. But when we got to New Zealand where the pitches were far more conducive to seam bowling and much more likely to produce results, I did not play until the last Test – and then it was on a pitch that was so flat that Geoff Howarth scored a century in both innings, Clive Radley batted more than eight hours for 158 and, even after six days, we were nowhere near a result, although it might have helped if I had not dropped two catches at deep square leg off successive balls from Ian Botham!

It did not register with me at the time but I did reflect later that I had played on all the flat pitches on that tour and none of the more sporting ones. But I could not complain. Maybe that was my value to the side, and, anyway, the bowlers who did play, expecially at Christchurch, where we levelled the series, did the job so the selectors had obviously made the right choices.

That was to remain my philosophy throughout my

England career. Willis, Botham, Old and Hendrick were all fine bowlers and it would have been presumptuous of me to say that I should have been playing all the time. After all, Willis and Botham were proven match-winners and if it was the selectors' judgement that Old and Hendrick were better bowlers than me, especially in English conditions, I could not argue with it.

I know that I was taking lots of wickets in the County Championship throughout those years but I do not think that I was ever a top-flight England bowler. I think I was a better-than-average county bowler who was fairly average at Test level. If it ever did cross my mind that I was being hard done by, I only had to look around the Essex changing-room at some of the very good cricketers who never even got a chance to play for England. People like Stuart Turner and Ray East would have given their right arms to have worn those three lions and a crown on their chests.

At the end of the day, a bowler is judged by the number of wickets he takes and I would have loved to have taken a hundred in Tests. That was a milestone that I fancied reaching and I sometimes wish that I had shown a bit more determination to get there.

I am not saying that I was the easiest player to leave out because I would always accept the situation and never moan about it, but perhaps there was a flaw in my make-up in that I did not push myself forward enough and demand more recognition. Perhaps I should have been a bit more like Ian Botham, who turned up at the Centenary Test in Melbourne as a virtually unknown youngster on a Whitbread Scholarship and told us all that he should be in the England side. He had not even made his mark in county cricket at the time but that attitude was to sweep him into the England team within a matter of months and make him the record-breaking cricketer that he is.

Still, as I have said, I never felt bitter or upset about the way my England career had gone and I was ready to accept that it was over when I got that offer to go to South Africa. No one can go on bowling for ever and, at the age of thirty-three, I was even beginning to wonder how much longer I could go on bowling for Essex because my knee had started to give me a few twinges.

I had had a handsome benefit in 1980 but I was still a long way from having the financial security I wanted outside the game, so the offer of a good deal of money to play for a South African Breweries team for no more than four weeks was very attractive and tempting.

It has since been revealed that the idea of an England side going to South Africa had been in the air for over a year. Apparently in February 1981, Geoff Boycott asked Ian Botham, David Gower, Graham Gooch, John Emburey and Graham Dilley to his hotel room in Guyana – ironically while the government there was preparing to serve a deportation order on Robin Jackman because of his South African links – to sound them out and there had been subsequent meetings in London the following autumn and in Bombay during the Indian tour.

But the whole thing was kept so secret that the first I knew about it was when that meeting was called in Colombo. Apart from Botham, Gower and Mike Gatting, who had all pulled out by then, bowlers like Dilley and Paul Allott had also said no, which is why I think I was invited. One or two others were still undecided – I well remember Derek Underwood saying that he would have to talk to his wife and Willis rounding on him angrily with the words: "Are you a man or a mouse?" – but I was keen to go for the reasons I have already outlined.

Keith Fletcher, I should emphasise, was not involved in any way, shape or form and I was under the impression that Gooch was not going to go, either, until I got home and received a phone call from him and his wife, Brenda,

79

saying that he had changed his mind. I remember thinking to myself at the time: "No, he shouldn't go . . . he's the next England captain."

I also had a call from Donald Carr, then secretary of the Test and County Cricket Board, which suggested that there had been a leak somewhere along the line, but by then I was as committed as anybody and just told him: "I don't want to tell any lies so I would rather not comment." And he was good enough to leave it at that.

The next day I reported to the hotel where we had been told to assemble and the first thing I noticed as I looked around the room was that Bob Willis was not there, having backed out at the very last moment. Geoff Cook did not turn up, either, so we were a couple of players short before we even set off, which tended to confirm my feeling that all I was doing was going on just another private cricket tour.

It was not until we actually got to South Africa that I realised it was a lot bigger than that. Our sponsors had called a press conference and from the look on one or two people's faces we immediately felt that we were being used in a way that none of us had quite envisaged. All the world's press – TV, radio reporters, newsmen – seemed to be there and you could feel the tension in the air as they played up the emotive subjects of cricket in South Africa and Apartheid.

The atmosphere really was quite frightening. Most of the players had not taken their wives with them and were generally concerned and upset by the media reaction and the effect it might have on them. We were called "The Dirty Dozen" – mercenaries who had only done it for the money and a disgrace to the game – and it was not long before the other wives were being flown out.

We did not think we had done anything to be ashamed of. Obviously we did go out there to make money, but we went to play cricket as well and you do not have to agree with Apartheid to do that. Whatever anyone else may have thought, we never felt that we were representing England. The South African players were given Springbok caps for playing in the three four-day games but, in all honesty, we did not even look like England. We did not wear England sweaters (I actually wore my Ilford Cricket Club sweater) and we did not have too many current England players but a mixture of the old, like Dennis Amiss, Alan Knott, Chris Old and Mike Hendrick, and the new, such as Les Taylor and Geoff Humpage. Graham Gooch, who we elected as our captain in preference to Geoff Boycott, had many an argument with scoreboard operators who invariably wanted to call us "An England XI" or even "*The* England XI". Gooch was forever pointing out that we were "The South African Breweries XI", but I am afraid it did not often say that on the scoreboard.

As for the cricket itself, I was very disappointed with the way it went and I think most of the other players felt the same. I had been to South Africa with Derrick Robins teams which had never won and was a bit fed up with them blowing their own trumpets and saying how good they were. But, although we trained hard, played hard and generally tried hard to give them a run for their money, we did not win a match.

We had not had much time to mould ourselves into a proper side and we ran into the usual problems that seem to afflict touring teams these days. We had a lot of arguments about the number of one-day games which did not give us an adequate build-up to the first four-day "Test" and we were not too impressed with some of the umpiring decisions.

But they were still good enough to beat us. Quite a few of them were playing county cricket – Clive Rice, Ken McEwan, Peter Kirsten, Garth Le Roux and Steve Jefferies – and some of the big names from the recent past

– Graeme Pollock, Barry Richards, Mike Procter and Vincent van der Bijl – were still around.

Graham Gooch played magnificently for us all the way through and Les Taylor was the find of the tour, bowling consistently well and sometimes quickly enough to hit a batsman as good as Pollock on the head. I think the rest of us let them down a bit. We never performed to our potential and played some pretty mediocre cricket. As for me, I was not particularly fit, probably through eating too many curries in India, where I had played only two Test matches in three months, and I did not find it much fun at all.

Then it was home to face the music. There were all sorts of stories circulating in Essex . . . members threatening to resign from the county club if Gooch and I stayed in the side, councillors at Southend trying to get Essex banned from playing at the municipal park, that kind of thing.

I found it all quite laughable really and in the end the fuss died down. Peter Edwards told me that the number of Essex members who did actually resign because of what we had done was almost equalled by the number who said they would resign if any action was taken against us so they just about cancelled each other out. And the only time I felt a stab of guilt about our clandestine activities was when Doug Insole came up to me and said: "I felt that we were close enough for you to have talked to me about it."

"I probably feel that way myself," I said, "but I was told that I must not say anything to anybody so I could not even say anything to you."

The fact was that I still did not feel that we had done anything wrong and I must say that I was shocked when the Test and County Cricket Board announced our punishment. I had always expected some kind of repercussions, but a three-year ban for going to South Africa to play cricket and earn our living seemed to be a savage sentence.

If we were endangering Test cricket, as some people claimed, then I suppose we deserved some kind of punishment but, to me, a three-year ban just did not seem to fit the "crime". And, like every English cricketer who goes out to South Africa, I was left wondering why cricket always seems to be the sport that has to suffer just because politicians cannot find other ways of getting back at the regime in South Africa.

As things turned out, I was to go back to South Africa for the next four winters, although that had nothing to do with the tour. Mike Procter was in charge of Natal in 1982–83 and after trying to sign several English seam bowlers but finding none of them available he turned to me as a last resort. I did not have a particularly good season but I made lots of friends in Durban, including a chap called Ernie Du Plessis, a South African who not only spoke Afrikaans but some of the tribal languages as well and had a deep understanding of the whole black-white situation.

Ernie became my sponsor and I went back to Durban to coach in various schools and at the university club, to play for Natal again in the floodlit limited-overs competition, which we won, and in 1985–86 to manage Natal, which was not without a few problems.

When I took the job, they were looking for a fast bowler and, knowing Graham Dilley's capabilities, I suggested that they signed him. But they were very sceptical about that.

"We've heard that his nickname's 'Picker'," they said, "because he picks and chooses his games."

"It's 'Picca', actually," I said. " 'Picca-Dilley'. Get it?"

In the end they signed him but Graham had an awful lot to do when he got there. He had to prove that he could bowl, he had to prove that he could stay fit and he had to prove that he was a good bloke. And he did it all in two weeks.

The first signs were not promising. In the nets he was bowling off a short run and his front foot was continually landing about a yard in front of the crease. And the captain and just about every other batsman who had found him a handful were soon getting on to me, saying: "You've got to do something about his no-balling or we're never going to get a game finished."

"Will you be all right when you get out in the middle?" I asked him.

"Yes," he said, "I think so."

He was, too, and after the first Currie Cup game in a season which was to bring him thirty wickets at only sixteen runs apiece they could not slap him on the back hard enough.

Graham was a credit to English cricket out there and I like to think the experience helped his rehabilitation in the Test side. He was also a great help to me in a difficult situation. I found that it was not very easy for an Englishman to manage a Currie Cup side. I did not get on very well with the captain, for a start, and later discovered that it was not always considered to be the done thing for the other players to listen to what I was saying.

Since I was not responsible for picking the side, either, I did not feel as though I was too much to blame when things went wrong, but the set-up was obviously not quite right and I said that I would not go back again if the same regime was still operating.

Unfortunately that was the case and I have not been back, but I have to say that I thoroughly enjoyed those four winters I spent out there and have many happy memories – and not just of the cricket.

I had got married in the summer of 1983 – to Chris, a girl I met during my first Test match in Delhi when she was working as an air hostess. We went out together for a while when I returned from India but I think life was a little bit too fast for me to settle down in those days. It was a few years later before we met up again at a Bob Willis benefit match, by which time she had been married but things had not worked out and we got together again.

And it was in Durban that our daughter, Jocelyn, was born in January 1985. Our son, James, came along in March 1988.

8

Seasons of Success

If somebody takes something away from you that you have cherished, or says that you can no longer do something that you have enjoyed doing, or even says that you are not good enough to do it any more, there is a tendency to think to yourself: "I'll show 'em." And, deep down in my sub-conscious, I suppose that is how I felt when I was banned from playing for England for three years for going to South Africa.

I do not know whether it was the severity of the punishment itself or the fact that some newspapers said that it did not really affect J. K. Lever because he was finished anyway, but something kept nagging away inside my head: "It's their loss not yours ... you show them that you can still bowl." Whatever it was, I took nearly 300 wickets in those three years and helped Essex to win two more County Championships and the John Player League.

Such success did not come immediately. I had returned from South Africa a bit overweight and feeling fairly unfit and, although I took seventy-two wickets in 1982, Essex did not have a particularly good season. As I have said, Keith Fletcher was bitterly disillusioned by his treatment from the England selectors and we lacked his usual brand of leadership as we struggled to seventh in the championship and did not get within striking distance in any of the one-day competitions.

The following season was different. I had lost a good deal of weight and got myself very fit in South Africa during the winter by doing a lot of running and, when Fletcher called us together to apologise for what had happened the year before and say, "Right, we're going to get stuck in this time," we were all ready to go.

As it happened, I made a false start. I missed some of the early matches because of a carbuncle on a toe: including that incredible game against Surrey when Nobby Phillip took six for four and they were skittled out for fourteen, the lowest score in their history and the best bowling performance in ours. No sooner had I got into my stride, however, than I went down with another, far more worrying complaint that took my mind off cricket completely for a while.

With apologies to the squeamish, what actually happened was that I had a kind of weeping from my navel which several doctors had a look at and diagnosed as various things from an ingrowing hair follicle to a hernia. Whatever it was, when I arrived at Southend to play against Hampshire it developed into a swelling the size of a cricket ball. I was bent double like an old man and could hardly walk as I was taken to hospital to see a surgeon, who took one look at it and said: "That's it. We're keeping you in tonight and I'll operate in the morning." It was diagnosed as a hiatus hernia.

I did not like the sound of that and he did say afterwards that if he had left it any longer it could have been very serious indeed. It was certainly the most uncomfortable experience of my life – yet, within a week, I was playing again in the Benson and Hedges Cup Final against Middlesex at Lord's.

Although the offending area still looked pretty dreadful and, most cricketers being fearful cowards when it comes to injuries, none of the lads would come near me in the dressing-room, I had been told that I could not do myself any more damage. But I think we had under-estimated the effects of the anaesthetic, which takes longer to disperse than anything else, and by the middle of that afternoon I felt very, very tired.

Having said that, we had bowled first and, despite a typical battling eighty-nine not out by Clive Radley, we had got ourselves a target of 197 which we thought we should be able to reach on a flat pitch. But after Graham Gooch and Brian Hardie had put on seventy-nine in eleven overs for the first wicket we collapsed from 127 for one to 196 all out. Naturally everyone was very disappointed, but I think I was the lowest of all. It was nearly nine o'clock by the time the match finished because of a delayed start and I felt absolutely drained.

That same complaint was to blow up again exactly a year later at Southend and I went straight back to see the surgeon. The swelling was not so big this time and he just lanced it, but I did have to go back into hospital at the end of that season for him to have a proper look. In the end it turned out that I needed only a smallish operation, but I remember thinking to myself: "This doesn't sound too good because it keeps coming back. What's going on?"

If it were to happen again now I think I would say: "It's the body telling you that you've had enough. Time to get out." But at that time I was still pretty fit, I still wanted to play cricket and I felt that I could carry on for a few more years.

I had missed a third of our matches in 1983 when the problem first erupted yet I still finished up with 106 first-class wickets as we put the disappointment of the Benson and Hedges Cup Final behind us and went on to

7. Keeping the lads' spirits up by making fools of ourselves on the 1976–77 Indian tour – Derek Randall, JKL, Mike Selvey and Geoff Miller. (*Light Shade Studio*)

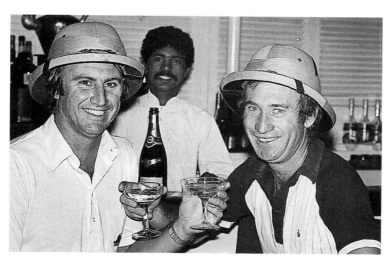

8. Keith Fletcher and I share a toast in India in 1981–82, little knowing that we were both on our last England tour.

9/10. Conflicting views on my ability from (above) Indian fans demonstrating over "the great Vaseline smear" at Madras in 1977 and (below) Essex supporters arriving at Lord's for our first final in 1979. (*Top, Adrian Murrell, Allsport*)

11. The strip of Vaseline gauze over the eyebrows which caused all the fuss. (*Adrian Murrell, Allsport*)

12. All is forgiven as the great motivator, Tony Greig, salutes the crowd at Bombay after clinching the series 3–1. (*Central Press*)

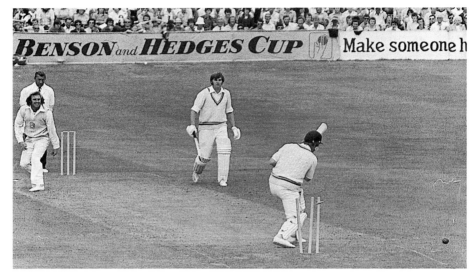

13/14. Swinging it both ways. An inswinger (above) accounts for
Yorkshire's Graham Stevenson in the Benson and Hedges Cup
semi-final at Chelmsford in 1979, while (below) Dilip Vengsarkar
edges an outswinger for Bob Taylor to claim another Test victim
at Bangalore on the 1981–82 Indian tour.
(*Below, Adrian Murrell, Allsport*)

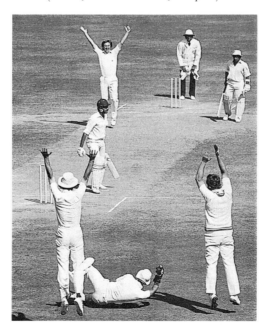

win the County Championship. I got another 116 wickets in 1984 when we won the Championship again and we won the John Player League as well to become the first team to land that particular double. I honestly believe that it was that three-year ban from international cricket – not so much on myself as on Graham Gooch – that helped us to do it.

We were not too bothered about what was happening on the Test match scene; we had the best batsman in England playing for us on a regular basis and, without being too big-headed about it, we found it relatively easy to win and keep on winning.

The other counties feared Gooch, and rightly so – especially in 1984 when he scored 2,559 runs, breaking the Essex record of 2,308 set up by Jack O'Connor fifty years earlier. But we also had Kenny McEwan, who got nearly 4,000 runs in those two seasons. With two such outstanding strikers of the ball at the height of their powers, we scored our runs so quickly that the bowlers' job was fairly straightforward. As in 1979, we always had attacking fields, and while you still have to bowl to them it does make life easier when every time you find the edge you get a wicket. That is what it was like for us and with that encouragement we simply steamrollered the opposition.

As for me, I was well past the tearaway stage that every fast or fast medium bowler goes through when too much energy is wasted on speculative balls such as the bouncer and the yorker. When you are young, your patience does not always measure up to what your brain is telling you to do and you get that surge of adrenalin which produces the big-effort ball – and, as often as not, a four or a six.

You can never know it all as a cricketer, but by the time you get to the age of thirty-four or thirty-five you do know enough to appreciate that bowling is all about what England manager Micky Stewart calls "putting the ball in the right channel" and having the patience to keep doing it consistently. The bouncer and the yorker do still come into play but they are not overdone, and I settled in to doing the job that I knew that I could do, which was running up and swinging the ball.

As I have appreciated throughout my career, bowling left-arm over was a great advantage, especially at a time when there were even fewer of my kind than there had been before. There were one or two youngsters still at the experimental stage, but county batsmen were not accustomed to facing somebody like me who had been doing it all his cricket life and had reached a certain level of performance.

In the meantime, the Essex side was gradually changing and it was the experience of players like Keith Fletcher, Stuart Turner, Ken McEwan and Keith Pont (who may not have been so celebrated but was still an important part of the set-up), plus, hopefully, myself which enabled us to go through the kind of transitional period that can be so traumatic to any club without losing too much of our momentum. It was done so subtly that there was a tendency for some cricket "experts" to think that the Essex players were growing old gracefully together, but that was not the case at all.

By the time we won the championship in 1983, Alan Lilley, Chris Gladwin, Derek Pringle, David East and Neil Foster had all begun to make their marks, and Paul Prichard appeared in 1984. So, despite the fact that Graham Gooch was back on Test duty in 1985, we were still able to complete another double, this time the NatWest Trophy and the John Player League, as well as reach the Benson and Hedges Cup Final and finish fourth in the championship.

We had what I think is essential to every successful side: a nucleus of experienced players who can help the younger ones come through. Also, all of a sudden, we had two new bowlers who were already playing for England, a new wicketkeeper who rapidly made a name for himself and several talented young batsmen who may not have gone straight to the top but were working away at the game and making steady progress.

The first of the newcomers to make a big impression, wicketkeeper David East, came into the side in the sort of situation that is always a little sad because the man he replaced, Neil Smith, was a very popular member of the side – and never more so than when he took that brilliant catch which had put us on the way to our first trophy in the Benson and Hedges Cup Final in 1979. But, unfortunately, he struck a patch when he just could not catch the ball cleanly behind the stumps.

For all his bulk – and he was a bit overweight – he had always had an excellent pair of hands, but it got to the stage when he came to me and said: "I feel as though I'm blinking every time the ball passes the bat and it finishes up on the ground." They stuck with him for a while but eventually it got so bad that he had to be dropped to the second team to try to sort things out.

That brought David East into the side and, quite frankly, he was a revelation – especially to me since I remembered him as a dumpy little batsman and occasional wicketkeeper who I had coached at the indoor school at Ilford when he was twelve. He had gone on to university and had spent a season on trial with Northamptonshire before coming back to us. Now he was very agile and caught just about everything standing back, but he still had quite a lot of work to do standing up to the stumps where Neil had been surprisingly good for a man of his build.

Unfortunately for Neil, such a technical consideration never really came into it. In only his second NatWest Trophy match against Gloucestershire, David held four catches, including a brilliant effort to dismiss the dangerous Zaheer Abbas, and was given the man of the match award. He never looked back after that, going on to win the Gordon's Gin Wicketkeeper of the Year award in 1983. Two years later, he set a world record by holding eight catches in one innings against Somerset – on his twenty-sixth birthday.

We had replaced one very good wicketkeeper with another and, while it was desperately unlucky for Neil, it did make people realise that Essex were not just an old boys' club. If you did not do well you were out, and I think that will always be the case in what has become a highly professional county.

Not that some people will believe that Essex are not an old boys' club when you get round to talking about Derek Pringle. Although he had been coming back from Cambridge University to play for us during the vacation for several years, he had already played in three Tests against India and had been selected for an England tour of Australia by the time we gave him his county cap. Even then some people felt it was a bit premature.

Actually, he had learned quite a lot, first under Gordon Barker, who had become the coach at Felstead School, and then up at Cambridge, where Brian Taylor was trying to instil some discipline into the undergraduates, but we knew – and, I am sure, he knew – that he still had to complete his cricket education when he came to us. It was not easy for him for various reasons.

One reason was that his arrival meant that there was another corner of the changing-room which we declared a "no go area". Previously, it had been only Ray East's kit that we avoided, but now there was another cricket bag that we had to put warning signs around because the socks did have a nasty habit of jumping out and attacking anybody who went past.

Another reason was that Keith Fletcher did not seem to be too sure who Pringle was. We had played Cambridge at Fenners and when Derek had come in to bat, Keith had said: "Who have we got here, then?"

"Oh, it's, er, Alastair Hignell," somebody told him.

To this day, Fletcher still calls Pringle "'Ignell". Though he claims it as a joke these days and probably does know the difference between our England all-rounder and Gloucestershire's former rugby inter-national, it is a fact that he never was too good with names. I remember that when he was captaining Eng-land in India and had to introduce the team at official receptions he always had a mental block when he came to Jack Richards and would say: "And this is . . . er . . . oh, yes . . . our reserve wicketkeeper!"

The third and rather more serious reason why Derek found it difficult to settle down as a county cricketer was his own laid-back attitude to life. He had had things fairly easy: England honours had come very quickly and, while he appreciated that and was never going to get too carried away with his Test status, he did have problems with the crowds and, to a degree, with the media. They seemed to resent the fact that a Cambridge Blue had been given the chance to play Test cricket without an awful lot of experience behind him, and he got quite a bit of stick.

He could hardly win with some sections of the press, which always seem to be saying that the selectors should blood more younger players and then, in the next breath, damning them when they do. And he could definitely not win with the crowds at every ground he played on. Even now, he still suffers because of what they consider to be his privileged treatment – and because of the fact that he is 6ft. 5in., 16½st., and not quite the most agile fielder in the country. In spite of all that, he still manages to ignore them all and give a hundred per cent every time he plays – and that is to his enormous credit.

I also happen to think that he is a very good cricketer. I have seen his bowling improve considerably over the past few years and I think he is very talented in that department, although he does struggle a little because of his size. His physical attributes help when it comes to hitting the deck hard and getting extra bounce, but he does have trouble maintaining his rhythm for long spells, especially when it is hot.

He would be the first to admit that his batting has not flourished quite as much as it should have done since those heady university days of 1982 when he scored 521 runs in six matches at an average of seventy-four, and opted to play for England in the second Test against India rather than the Varsity match. He is capable of being a very aggressive player and turning a match with an explosive twenty-minute knock, and I am sure that we will see more innings like that the longer he plays. But I still do not think that he has quite worked out how to bat to his full potential. It is something the Essex players are always nagging him about.

In stark contrast to Pringle, it is the lack of meat on Neil Foster's slender 6ft. 4in. frame that has dogged him throughout a career which began amid great excitement on my own Ilford ground in 1980. He had been summoned from school on his eighteenth birthday to play against Kent because we were so short of players through illness, and I well remember his debut – probably because I saw another Lever in the making.

He was raw but he was definitely quick and full of potential. After his first ball had gone for four wides he bowled well enough on a typically slow Valentine's Park pitch to get some good players out, Bob Woolmer and Chris Tavare among them. There was a buzz among the Essex players and members that night because we had found another bowler of more than average ability.

However, it was to be a long time before he was able to fulfil that high promise. He began to suffer from back trouble when he went to Tasmania on a Whitbread

Scholarship, and his back was virtually coming apart when he went into hospital in September 1982 for a major operation in which two six-inch metal plates were inserted to hold it together.

I had seen what the lad was going through that summer when we played Lancashire at Liverpool. I was injured myself and was in the changing-room when he broke down yet again and had to come off. And I felt really sorry for him because he thought that his career was over.

The operation was successful enough for him to make his Test debut against New Zealand at Lord's the following season but, by then, one of the screws securing those metal plates had worked loose and within a week he was back in hospital having the plates and two abscesses removed. With all that to cope with, it says much for his character that he was back in the England side for that winter's tour of New Zealand and Pakistan and, although it took him quite a long time, he had now established himself as our number one bowler alongside Graham Dilley.

When you see Foster in the changing-room, there is nothing of him. He is built like a drink of water and his clothes literally hang on him. But he does have that something extra, the desire to succeed and the will to win, which has made him into a top bowler. All the ingredients are there. He has a lovely high action, sufficient pace to make even the best batsmen think, and the ability to put the ball in the right place – and there is a batting side to him as well.

We picked that up very early on at Essex. His speciality was the big, flowing, front-foot drive of the coached schoolboy, but he always hit the ball very hard and now he has learned to play a few other shots as well. He is not all that strong and he will always have problems with injury, but if he can overcome them as well as he has done so far he is going to win a lot more games for years to come – with bat as well as ball.

When it came to specialist batsmen, we had one major disappointment. Chris Gladwin, a big, strapping left-hander from East Ham, came into the side with all the confidence of modern youth and made such an impact in his first full season in 1984 that he scored nearly 1,400 runs, was awarded his county cap and was even talked of as a possible England player. He was so full of himself that he would stand a foot outside the crease to even the fastest bowlers and take them all on, although he did get a crack on the head one day when Malcolm Marshall took exception to such a cavalier approach.

It is the second season, though, that tends to sort out a young batsman and, unfortunately Chris did not seem to knuckle down and apply himself to the task of becoming a professional cricketer. There was no doubt that he had heaps of talent but for three years the runs were not forthcoming and in the end the club decided to let him go and he was released at the end of the 1987 season.

Now everybody in Essex is looking to Paul Prichard to be our next England batsman – and I do not think that they will be disappointed despite a severe finger injury that has set him back probably a couple of years. That happened at Chelmsford at the start of the 1987 season when Warwickshire fast bowler Allan Donald bowled him a high full toss in poor light which he just did not see. It shattered the middle finger of his right hand. Like Neil Foster before him, Paul thought that he career was over, but more metal-work eventually put his finger together again and by 1988 he had rehabilitated himself with more than 1,000 runs in the season.

He is an unassuming bloke but for one so young he has been around quite a bit. He joined Essex when he was only sixteen and was soon having beer poured over him by the captain when he happened to mention in the pub that Keith Fletcher had made his first-class debut three years before he was born. Actually, he has one or two of Keith's mannerisms about him, especially in the way he walks to the wicket, and he has worked just as diligently at his game.

Paul is also like a whippet in the field and his arrival certainly enhanced our one-day performances. Batsmen were beginning to push the ball towards one or two of us older players, but once we got Prichard on one side of the wicket and Alan Lilley on the other such liberties were not taken.

I had a special interest in Alan Lilley because he was an Ilford boy and mirrored the way I had come through into country cricket. He had been coached at the Ilford school by Bill Morris and Stuart Turner – whom he always called "dad" – and later coached there himself like I had done. And there was plenty of mickey-taking when we played at Valentine's Park. In the old days, Ilford probably felt that they were as good as any county side and there is still plenty of good-natured rivalry when Essex play there. I am always raising the Ilford flag and with good reason, I believe, because of the number of good players who have come through our system.

Alan is certainly one of them but, although he scored a century on his debut against Nottinghamshire in 1978, it was to be another eight years before he finally got his cap. Because we had some superb batsmen, he was in and out of the side like Keith Pont had been and his batting suffered from that. He would turn up at the ground not knowing whether he was in the team, twelfth man or about to be dispatched to play for the 2nd XI. And, being a sensitive sort of lad, his confidence was affected.

It was only when he was in the field that he felt completely at home and his fielding became a significant factor in Essex winning quite a few one-day competitions. Some of us felt that it was so important that both Graham

Gooch and I had been to see the chairman asking if he could be given his cap two years before he actually got it. Our request was turned down on the grounds that he still had to earn it in first-class cricket, but I think that is wrong because the one-day game has become so much a part of the overall picture.

He did eventually get his cap and the way it was done made it a very emotional moment for everybody. It was well known that John Childs was going to be capped at the end of the 1986 season because he had bowled magnificently and been largely instrumental in our winning the Championship again. We all gathered on the pavilion balcony as Graham Gooch went out, cap in hand, and made the presentation.

The other players had been briefed about what would happen next but Alan was completely in the dark and his face was a picture of misery until Peter Edwards, who had made the announcement on the public address, added: "And now Graham has another pleasant duty to perform which is to present a cap to Alan Lilley . . ."

From underneath his sweater, Graham produced a second cap and tears rolled down Alan's face as he went to receive it. He had been with us for so long that he must have been thinking that it would never happen.

Just how much Lady Luck plays her part in that sort of thing was perfectly illustrated by the fairy-tale story of John Childs, who had been with Gloucestershire for ten years and got his cap there as long ago as 1977 before he even joined Essex at the age of thirty-four.

Ray East had decided in 1983 that he had had enough. He had ducked his last bouncer and, seeing a niche as captain and coach of the second team in succession to Mike Denness which would not be left unfilled for much longer, he decided that that was what he wanted to do. I think that everybody at the club was reluctant to let him do it because we all wanted him to carry on playing, but he had made up his mind and seized the job with both hands.

That left us without a slow left armer and when we went down to play at Bristol the following summer I approached John Childs, at Keith Fletcher's request, and said: "How are things going for you here?"

"Well," he replied, "with David Graveney [another left-arm spinner] captaining the side I should really be thinking about moving on because I can't see myself playing in too many games."

We knew his capabilities because he had already taken five wickets in an innings twenty-one times and we knew that "Charlie" would fit nicely into the Essex set-up as he is such a likeable bloke, so the wheels were set in motion for him to join us in 1985.

He was not an instant success. In fact he took only three wickets at a cost of 125 runs apiece in his first year with us and expected to be given the sack when our chairman, Doug Insole, asked to see him at the end of that season. On the contrary, Doug and Keith Fletcher wanted him to try to overcome what is a rare fault among spinners these days – bowling *too* slowly – and that winter he spent several sessions in the Indoor School at Lord's with Fred Titmus and Don Wilson, the MCC coach and himself a slow left armer for Yorkshire and England.

The outcome in 1986 was a straighter, longer run-up, a quicker flight and eighty-five wickets at an average of fifteen, more than half of them coming in the last few weeks of the season as we came from fifty-four points behind the leaders to win the championship by twenty-eight points. I well remember him being very emotional about it all.

"It might not mean too much to you boys," he said, "because you've done this kind of thing before – but it's the first time I've won the championship."

He was wrong in one respect because it did mean just

as much to all of us, I can assure you. Graham Gooch, who had taken over the captaincy, missed a lot of matches on England duty; Keith Fletcher and Brian Hardie missed several games through injury and Stuart Turner played only once; but a huge team effort saw us through. But, having had to wait so long to win the championship ourselves, we could quite understand his feelings.

Yet that was only the beginning of the fairy tale as far as Charlie was concerned. From then on he continued to perform to such a high standard for us that in 1988 he was called up to play for England at the age of thirty-seven. Again luck had a big part to play because Nick Cook of Northamptonshire was the original selection for the third Test against the West Indies at Old Trafford, but he turned his ankle on a boundary rope in a county match – and when he was only twelfth man at that – and had to withdraw. So Charlie got his chance and I doubt if there was a cricketer in the country who was not delighted for him. He did not get too many wickets but he bowled well enough to be chosen for the winter tour to India – and if it was sad for everybody when that trip and the subsequent alternative in New Zealand had to be called off then it was almost tragic for him because at his age he was not going to get many more opportunities to tour with England.

Geoff Miller, of course, had been on any number of England tours when he joined us from Derbyshire in 1987, but his ability was questioned a little when he did not get too many runs or too many wickets in his first season. He had not been happy with Derbyshire for some time but he had problems trying to play for a county in the south while his family was still up north, a situation which was never going to be easy for him. Yet I thought he stuck to his job pretty well and whenever we did get on a turning pitch he and John Childs usually produced the goods.

At least he was another player who was soon very much at home in the Essex changing-room. I had roomed with him many times on tour and he was also fairly close to Keith Fletcher and Graham Gooch. And I cannot stress too strongly the importance of such togetherness in the Essex scheme of things.

We have been just as fortunate in our overseas players starting with Keith Boyce and going on to Lee Irvine, Bruce Francis, Nobby Phillip, Kenny McEwan and, in 1986, to Allan Border, who surprised us all by the way he became an Essex man from the moment that he set foot on the ground at Chelmsford.

We knew that he would have to leave a month before the end of the season to captain Australia in India, but by the time he left, his 1,400 runs had had a lot to do with getting us in contention for our third championship in four years, which we eventually won with a match to spare.

In less than four months he had become very much a part of the Essex scene and we missed him very much when he was unable to return in 1987. This was despite the fact that we felt that we had signed another more than useful replacement as our overseas player in Hugh Page, a South African fast medium bowler who could also bat a bit, in the face of some pretty fierce competition, most notably from Nottinghamshire, whose captain, Clive Rice, obviously rated him quite highly.

I had seen Page play under Rice in the South African side and I thought that he was a good bowler, very quick, very straight and capable of swinging the ball away. What we did not know was that he had not been bowling that way in Currie Cup cricket and we soon discovered why. He was favouring an injury to his front knee which needed an operation at the end of what turned out to be his only season with us.

We were sorry to see him go because, once again, he

had proved to be a smashing bloke, but our disappointment eased when we found out that Allan Border had agreed to come back again in 1988. That season with Hugh Page had convinced us that we needed somebody who could score a few more runs rather than another seam bowler and, if anything, "AB" played better than he had done before, scoring another 1,400 runs and again leaving us with a chance of winning the title.

This time we could not quite make it – probably because of a highly eventful Colchester week when we lost to Nottinghamshire by two wickets off the last ball of the match and then drew with Glamorgan with the scores level – and finished third, eight points behind the champions, Worcestershire. And at the end of the season some people were again beginning to suggest that Essex were on the decline.

We had not won anything for two years which was, I suppose, pretty mediocre by our standards and we were going through another period of restructuring. But I thought that we still had a strong enough nucleus of senior players to help the younger ones through and ensure that we would continue to have a side capable of winning things.

It is not often talked about when a county's prospects are under discussion but I think that one of the most important aspects, probably *the* most important aspect, is to have players in reserve who are capable of coming into the first team and playing an innings or bowling a spell that is going to win a game. We have been lucky to have such players over the years in people like Keith Pont and Alan Lilley, who may not always have held down regular places but have been an essential part of Essex's success.

As I write, we are obviously looking to Mark Waugh, twin brother of Steve, the Australian Test player who had such an outstanding season with Somerset in 1988, to build on the promise that he has already shown and prove himself to be a worthy successor to Allan Border. But we are also looking to our home-grown players to come through and maintain the strength of our first-team squad.

Some of them have already begun to make names for themselves. John Stephenson, another of Gordon Barker's boys from Felstead School, was the first captain of the Combined Universities side when he was at Durham and clearly has lots of ability as an opening batsman. He has a nice sense of humour, too, but he takes his cricket very seriously and he does get a little bit too upset when he loses his wicket.

Our scorer, Clem Driver, tells of the time when he made a long car journey with him and it was two hours before John said a word. "I thought somebody had died or something," said Clem, "but when I finally asked him what was troubling him he said that he was upset about getting out."

That was fairly understandable when he got out within one run of his first championship century against Leicestershire at Chelmsford, but sometimes he needs Keith Fletcher or somebody to put things in the right perspective for him. I am certain it is something that can be corrected.

Don Topley hit the headlines in 1984 when he was on the MCC groundstaff and went on as twelfth man for England against the West Indies at Lord's, brilliantly "catching" Malcolm Marshall one-handed on the square-leg boundary only to put one foot over the rope. He went on to play for Surrey in 1985 but preferred to join Essex instead as the prospective successor to Stuart Turner. I am sure he has the ability to fill that role because he has never let us down when he has come into the side and was rewarded for his sixty-five wickets in 1988 with his county cap.

Ian Pont, younger brother of Keith, is more famous for

his baseball-pitching in the United States, where he had trials for the legendary New York Yankees, than he is for his fast bowling, but he can make the grade if he knuckles down to some hard work. Nasser Hussain is such an accomplished young batsman that Keith Fletcher stood down from quite a few games in 1988 to give him the chance to play with Allan Border and gain valuable experience.

Nasser is a particularly exciting prospect to me because he is one of the three cricketing sons of Jainad (or Joe, to us) Hussain, who is the current captain of Ilford. And I also have a certain interest in the progress of Mark Ilott, who joined us from Hertfordshire and just happens to be a left-arm swing bowler.

Whether they go on to establish themselves in the first team or not, it is crucial for Essex to keep people like them happy and involved and ready to step in when we lose players through Test calls and injuries.

Most sides cannot do that and the disenchanted back-up players leave to try their luck with other counties, but Essex have a good record in that respect. It may have something to do with the environment we have created, which is why I am delighted to say that the atmosphere in our changing-room has not changed too much for all the comings and goings over the past twenty years.

These days we tend to sit back and listen to the non-stop banter that goes on between Derek Pringle and Neil Foster, who are for ever arguing about their batting, their bowling and their fielding – and sometimes swapping insults in a fairly personal vein.

"If you weren't sixteen-and-a-half stone and carrying so much overweight, you'd have been able to cut off that boundary," Foster will tell his sometime England colleague.

"Don't talk to me about my body when yours looks the

way it does," Pringle will respond. "You can't even go near magnets!"

They get on very well, really, but we do get constant amusement just listening to those two having a go at each other – especially since we know that "Fozzy" tends to bite a bit too often and "Pring" can always be guaranteed to have the last word. Unless he happens to drag Alan Lilley into the debate...

Lilley is a bit like Ian Botham in that his humour – and his response to any argument he looks like losing – is purely physical and, again like Botham, he is so strong that he has even been known to pick up Pringle and deposit him in the bath!

9

Who Was
That Lady?

Who was that lady I saw you with last night? If anybody
had bumped into Ian Botham one crisp winter morning
at Jammu in Northern India in December 1981 and
asked him that time-honoured question, he could have
replied in all honesty: "That was no lady ... that was
John Lever!"

Perhaps I had better explain. We had travelled to
Jammu, one of the farthest outposts of first-class cricket
bordering Kashmir in the foothills of the Himalayas,
from Delhi via Chandigarh where the Indian Airlines
pilot got more bounce from the runway than we got out of
the wickets throughout the entire tour.

On arrival at our hotel, we discovered that our beds
were damp and the only solution was to leave the
mattresses propped in front of the single-barred electric
fires all day while we went off to play the match against
North Zone. In the evenings, the only diversion was the
rumbling convoy of what the press solemnly assured us
were Russian-built tanks rolling towards the India-
Pakistan border.

It is in this kind of situation that touring cricketers
have got to make their own entertainment to keep their

spirits up. And when Ian Botham, Geoff Miller and myself noticed that "A Grand Dance" was being held in our own hotel we seized our opportunity.

"Dusty" Miller went off to the local bazaar by buy an assortment of ladies' clothes, a wig and make-up, I was deputed (don't ask me why!) to get dressed up and "Both" prepared to escort me to the ball. I felt a bit of an idiot, to be honest, but the joke went down well in the team room, where none of the other players had known anything about it.

Then, fortified by a couple of beers, it was downstairs to the dance on Ian's arm and, despite one or two odd looks from the other guests, it was all good fun . . . until an Indian chap decided that he wanted to dance with me. He just would not take "no" for an answer and in the end I had to get my escort to tell him: "Leave her alone . . . she's with me!"

Ian's humour was always rather more physical than Geoff's and mine but at least we were always on the same wavelength as far as pranks were concerned. They probably seem childish to anyone who was not there at the time but touring teams do need people who are willing to put themselves out a little bit to get a laugh somewhere along the line.

Particularly in countries like India and Pakistan, it is so easy for players to moan if things are not going well, to moan if they are bored, to moan if the food is bad, to moan about everything under the sun. And I believe that players who are prepared to take a little trouble to stop the moaning are worth a lot to the side.

Geoff Miller, who went on six England tours between 1976 and 1983, was always one of those players and, apart from sharing rooms, we also shared the same sense of humour. The hardest time to be away is at Christmas when players can just sit around thinking that they would rather be at home with their wives and families or just down at the pub. One year Goeff and I decided to try to take their minds off things.

We went out shopping and bought presents for everyone in the party – just little things which we thought were appropriate and would get a laugh when they were unwrapped. I cannot remember them all but there was a huge plastic comb for Geoff Boycott, a miniature first-aid kit for Chris Old, a toy monkey on a trapeze for our physiotherapist, Bernard Thomas, who had been a gymnast in his younger days and still liked to show us what he could do around the swimming-pool, and a whole series of those *Mister Man* books, including *Mr Noisy* for David Bairstow.

Again, it sounds schoolboyish now but we got through that Christmas Day without too much homesickness – and I like to think that it helped us to go out and beat Australia in the World Series Cup on Boxing Day.

Since those days, of course, the off-the-field activities of England cricketers have made much more lurid headlines than our little pranks ever did. The only times I can remember cricket getting on to page one of the newspapers when I was touring between 1976 and 1982 was with stories concerning the game itself, like the Vaseline row, the Packer affair, the strike threat in Pakistan and the "rebel" tour to South Africa. Nowadays, hardly a tour seems to go by without some kind of drinks, drugs or sex allegations.

I find it all rather sad because I do not think that today's players behave any differently than they ever did in relation to the society they happen to live in. Nor do I believe that the average spectator is too worried about what they do in their private lives as long as it does not affect the way they play. But other people will say that if you are in the public eye then your private life is not your private life any more, and I am afraid that there is no arguing with that.

Cricket reflects how attitudes have changed in that respect. When you are away on tour for three or four months there are bound to be nights when there is nothing to do, you are a little bit bored and you go out and have a few drinks. But looking back to my touring days, I seem to recall that on the occasions when we did have one or two too many it was invariably in the company of the press. And they knew that if we were slightly over the top, we would work that much harder the next morning to get ourselves back in shape.

It is easy to become bored on the subcontinent where play finishes at 5.30 p.m. because it gets dark so early and there is nothing to look forward to apart from the evening meal. For those who do not like spicy food that is not too much of a highlight, either.

Most of the diversions that stick in my memory now seem pretty mundane, really, although they seemed like adventures at the time – such as the evening when I joined two of my cricket-writing friends on a trip from Bombay's airport hotel, where we were staying overnight, into the city centre. We decided to go by train and, after joining what seemed to be the entire population of India on the station platform, we made the journey on the *outside* of the carriage, clinging grimly to the person in front of us but in absolutely no danger of falling off because of the pressure from behind. Commuting into London has never held any terrors for me after that.

More exotic was the experience of Derek Underwood, who was given a couple of days off when we were playing up country to accompany Tony Greig to Goa, the resort paradise where the playboys and playgirls go around the beach bottomless as well as topless.

"We might as well join 'em, Deadly," said Greigy, whipping off his shorts after they had gone only a few yards – but the great bowler, modest as ever, declined to conform.

What has caused so many problems for the England players in more recent years is that, whereas we were only accompanied by *bona fide* cricket correspondents who had the interests of the game at heart and with whom we shared a mutual respect and a common interest in keeping each other sane, nowadays touring teams are pursued by a press corps containing far more newsmen than genuine cricket-writers who are interested only in finding a story – and the juicier the better.

Just imagine what they would have made of the England captain walking along an Indian beach in the nude ... or of an escapade involving some of the Essex players a few years ago when Keith Boyce jumped on a bed during a bout of horseplay in a hotel room and smashed it. At midnight, there were three of us – Ray East, Robin Hobbs and myself – carrying a broken bed down two flights of stairs and replacing it with a bed from another room which we proceeded to carry back up the stairs.

As it turned out, we did not get away with it because once we assembled the new bed we discovered that it was a different height from the other one and we were soon found out the next morning. And our captain, the worldly-wise Brian Taylor, was naturally sceptical about our explanation.

"Think I came over on the last banana boat, do you?" he challenged his young charges – which did not seem to be the most tactful thing to say in front of our Barbadian colleague.

"Honestly, Tonker, that's all that happened," we pleaded.

And honestly that is all there was to it. But I am sure that today's press would have a field-day if they got hold of a story like that.

I can only come to the conclusion that I was lucky to have been an England player when I was instead of having to look over my shoulder all the time as the players do now, just in case somebody is watching and might misconstrue what is actually going on. Indeed I treasure the memories of my England tours and I am sure that most players who are lucky enough to have been on them feel the same – despite the perils that entrap every side in some parts of the world.

My worst bout of illness was in Pakistan where, despite feeling unwell on the journey by plane and bus across the Sind desert to Hyderabad, I somehow struggled through to the rest day in the Test match before taking to my bed. There I lay for hour after hour feeling dreadful, shivering and sweating and fighting back the awful feeling of nausea until my room-mates, Ian Botham and Bob Willis, came in with a bottle of brandy.

"Come on," they said, "sit up and take a glass of this. It will settle your stomach."

"Oh, no," I groaned, "I can't stand brandy. It tastes like medicine."

"You've got to take it," ordered Doctor Botham, pouring out a generous measure and obviously in no mood for an argument. I took one sip and shot straight out of bed into the bathroom where I was suddenly being more sick than I have ever been in my life – to the accompaniment of laughter from the bedroom and a chorus of: "Go on, it's the best thing for you."

They were right, too. I had felt as though I was dying all day but, although I still felt a bit weak the next morning, I was otherwise all right and I was soon bowling again in the Test match.

You never forget incidents like that and such friendships as I struck up with people like Geoff Miller, Ian Botham, Bob Willis, Wayne Larkins and many more obviously add to the enjoyment of playing county cricket. You have friends in most sides and look forward to seeing them again. Yet, even without those special relationships, I have always found the county circuit a wonderful place to earn a living.

From the start, I found that there were certain sides who I really enjoyed playing against, Lancashire were one of them. They had players like Harry Pilling, John Sullivan, Ken Shuttleworth, Keith Goodwin, David Lloyd and David Hughes – all blokes who seemed to enjoy playing their cricket and having a bit of fun.

Glamorgan were another team with whom we seemed to hit it off pretty well. They had a good side in those days – in fact they won the championship in 1969 – with men like Don Shepherd, Peter Walker, Tony Lewis, Roger Davis, Alan Jones, Tony Cordle and Malcolm Nash, who were always prepared to pass the time of day with you. I will never forget the thrill I got when we played Nottinghamshire and Garry Sobers came across to have a few words. As a youngster bowling left arm, I had always idolised him and the mere fact that he knew my name meant an awful lot to me. I remember thinking to myself at the time: "This isn't going to be a bad life at all."

There have been the odd occasions when I have had my doubts. One was the day Peter Marner, a mighty striker of a cricket ball with first Lancashire and then Leicestershire, hit me for six fours in one over at Grace Road. As I took my sweater, he came down the wicket and said: "Sorry, son."

"What did he say?" barked our captain, Brian Taylor, dashing up from behind the stumps.

"He said he was sorry," I muttered sheepishly.

"Cheeky bugger," snarled Tonker, scuttling away without a word of sympathy himself.

Another was the time that the car windscreen shattered just as we were crossing the Severn Bridge on our way from Swansea to Eastbourne, which is not the easiest of journeys at the best of times. We had to keep going and there were some curious looks from the holiday-makers as four Essex players drove into the Sussex resort on a balmy summer's evening huddled in sweaters, scarves, duffel coats and anything else warm that we could find in the boot – yet still wearing sunglasses to protect our eyes.

Then there was the night that we turned up at an hotel in Birmingham's Hagley Road to find Raymond East pacing up and down the lobby in obvious distress. "I don't think much to this place," he complained as we came through the door.

"What's the matter with it?" I asked.

"It's a temperance hotel," he gasped, his tongue hanging out like an overworked sheepdog's. "No bar. Dry."

We solved that problem by quenching our thirst down the road and bringing back a seven-pint pipkin which we placed in the wash basin so that we could have a drink when we got back in the evenings. It was in the days when the county was trying to save a bit of money, but we never stayed there again. We were already sleeping three and four in a room but a temperance hotel was just too much.

Social drinking has always been part of cricket life, of course, and Essex are as good at it as most counties. It does not seem to have done us a lot of harm and, in any case, all that chatting over a pint or three is a valuable source of information, especially if you are a bowler.

Nowadays we are often invited into the sponsors' boxes or tents for drinks after the day's play and our hosts must sometimes think it is a bit rude of the players to huddle together and talk among themselves. But it is a chance to catch up with the players you have toured with or played against over the years and find out how they are faring, how the family is getting on and how the benefit preparations are going. And, naturally, the talk soon turns to cricket.

That is when you keep your ears open for the odd

remark about who they have been playing against recently. "You wouldn't pitch too many up to him," or, "It's a waste of time having a cover for him," or, "Third slip might come in handy for him," or, "He got a hundred against us and sixty per cent of his runs went through midwicket." You never actually sit down and discuss how to get a particular batsman out but, without labouring any point too much, you pick up little snippets which can be useful.

There is hardly any wonder that one of cricket's truisms is that the second season is always the hardest for any young batsman, no matter how well he might have done in his first. This is partly due to the grapevine, although in most well-run sides we have a fair idea about how any newcomer is going to play before we have even seen him.

This is where your own young players from the second team can play a big part. They will invariably have played against him in 2nd XI cricket and I will always have a word with one or two of our boys before we go out on to the field and say: "How does this chap play? Where does he score most of his runs? What's his favourite shot?"

Armed with that information, you should have some kind of mental picture after you have bowled a couple of overs at him so that by the time Keith Fletcher, or whoever the captain happens to be, comes down the pitch to have a word about the field placing the whole thing has come together.

That kind of thing is even more important in the one-day game than it is in the championship. Limited-overs are so tight that two overs spent finding out whether a bloke is stronger on the front foot or the back can cost you runs that you cannot afford so you really need to know about him from the outset. It can be quite nerve-wracking for a bowler to have to run up and bowl against a new batsman who he has never seen play before and try to work him out from scratch.

However friendly county cricket may seem from the outside, it is more competitive now than it has ever been and absolutely nothing is given away. And that is the way it should be.

As a side, we at Essex have had some pretty diabolical declarations made against us which have not given us the remotest chance of winning simply because we have been so successful in recent years, but that is the sort of thing that you have to expect when you are successful. Whenever it happens, Keith Fletcher is the first one to turn round and say: "There's no point bitching about it. If you can bowl sides out twice, you don't have to worry about declarations."

We now accept that when we turn up at any county ground we are not going to get any favours. We are going to have to make all the running if we want to win. But, in saying that, I am not running down any opposition captain. If we were playing against a side that was as successful as we have been we would probably adopt the same attitude.

Yet while success may have meant that other counties see Essex in a different light, I do not think that it has changed the way we see ourselves too much. Stuart Turner is no longer around to scan the newspapers at breakfast time for any one-day scores of 200 and over so that he could gleefully read out the figures of the unfortunate bowlers. David Acfield is no longer there to join Keith Fletcher in exploring the delights of the best English, French and Italian cuisine in the area where we happen to be playing. And Stuart and Ray East no longer accompany Brian Hardie and Alan Lilley to the local hamburger joint or hot dog stall to form a fast food team which Fletch used to call "the scum eaters".

"How can you play cricket on that?" he would ask. But

it was what they liked to do – and it did mean spending a lot less time away from the bar!

Beer drinking, I have to admit, remains our favourite recreation – although I should add that there is more emphasis on quality than quantity, especially since Derek Pringle began to exert more and more influence on our social activities. Pring is a connoisseur of real ale. He can quote the specific gravity of even the most obscure beers from little-known breweries and knows which ones have won what awards at the various festivals.

He will go out of his way to find the Frog and Parrot, or whatever it might be, in Sheffield or somewhere and lead us off to some of the grottiest pubs – or, as he would describe them, "most alternative" pubs – you have ever seen. It does not bother him if there is sawdust on the floor or the place seems to have been taken over as the headquarters for all the bikers from miles around who might take exception to a tall, bespectacled Cantabrian walking in followed by a strange assortment of blokes wearing Essex ties and blazers. We are only there for the beer as far as he is concerned and all that matters is that they serve a good pint – but we do make sure that we take Alan Lilley with us, even though he will not sample the real ale but will stick to his habitual lager. He is as tough as any of the pubs we visit and the watchword is always: "Keep your glasses on, Pring, and make sure that Lill's standing behind you."

Then, for an increasing number of us, it is off for an Indian curry to keep us going for another day. And God help the changing-room the next morning!

10

The Gooch
Phenomenon

By now you may be thinking that in my assessment of the Essex teams and players with whom I have been associated I have not given enough credit to the enormous contribution made by one Graham Alan Gooch. But there is a simple reason for that: it is because I want to try to give you a deeper insight into a player who, for all his shyness and dislike of personal publicity, has become one of the most controversial cricketers in the world over the past few years.

To understand the Gooch phenomenon, you have to appreciate that he is absolutely single-minded – as we discovered at Essex before he had even joined the county staff. He was a contemporary of Keith Pont in his schooldays and, although they showed equal promise at the time, we were all a little surprised when Keith joined us a year before Graham did. "Why haven't they signed Goochy?" everyone was asking because, even then, we felt that he was a bit special.

It turned out that it had been nothing to do with the club. Graham had been adamant that he was going to complete his four-year apprenticeship as a toolmaker with a small firm near his home at Leytonstone before embarking on a career as precarious as a professional sportsman's. There was very little chance that he would have to earn his living as a toolmaker ever again but he wanted to have something to fall back on just in case he did not make the grade as a cricketer.

He had started playing for Ilford at a time when I was away from the club more than at any stage of my career and I did not play with him very often there. But I well remember him turning up for nets – on his motor scooter. With his short hair-cut, his long parka and his thick-soled shoes, he was very much what we used to call a "mod" in those days. Yet he had an old-fashioned approach to playing cricket. All he wanted to do was whack the ball as hard as he could and when I visited Ilford one day, someone said to me: "Have you heard about Goochy?"

"No," I said. "What's he done?"

"Well," he said, "we played a twenty-overs game against Wanstead and he scored 175 all on his own . . . not out!"

I bowled at him myself a few times in the indoor school under the watchful eye of Bill Morris and I will never forget the look on the coach's face when I pitched the ball on leg stump and Graham flipped it in the direction of square leg with all the time in the world. I would turn round and walk back, thinking to myself: "Blimey, that wasn't a bad shot." And there would be Bill, standing behind the stumps with his arms folded, a big grin on his face and his eyebrows raised as if to say: "This bloke can play, can't he?" I would just nod in agreement.

Graham, who is more than four years younger than me, would have been about eighteen then and he was twenty by the time he played for Essex. He came into the side at number seven, which I think is always the best way to introduce a new young batsman, but gradually we pushed him up the order to number four or five and within two years he was making his Test debut for England against Australia.

I do not think anybody at Essex was too surprised by his selection. He had always seemed destined to play for England because he was already capable of taking the bowling apart and winning a match in any class of cricket. However, it was asking a bit much of him to take on Dennis Lillee and Jeff Thomson, who had just spent the winter terrorising England's batsmen in Australia, and he had a traumatic start to his Test career in two matches which turned out to be Mike Denness' last as England captain and Tony Greig's first.

Graham got a "pair" at Edgbaston, surviving only three balls in the first innings and seven in the second, as England crashed to an innings defeat. But there were extenuating circumstances. Mike Denness, perhaps fearful of what Lillee and Thomson might do, gambled in the face of a weather forecast predicting rain and paid the ultimate price when his batsmen were caught on a wet pitch. And for Graham, very much the new boy in a batting order that started with John Edrich, Dennis Amiss, Keith Fletcher and Denness and had Greig and Alan Knott to follow, it was a nightmare.

He did rather better at Lord's, where Greig raised England's morale with a typically defiant ninety-six, making only six in the first innings but scoring thirty-one in the second. At least he had begun to look the part of a Test batsman, but it could not quite erase the memory of those two ducks and it was to be another three years before he played for England again – as an opener.

Everybody told him that he was not an opening batsman. Some people still say that he isn't. But he realised that the position was becoming available in the Essex side, he saw an opportunity for himself and he worked so hard on his technique that he not only made himself into an opening batsman but he made himself into one of the best in the world.

When you see him playing now, it is easy to run away with the idea that he has always played that way. But if you look at the video-recordings of his early Tests, you will see that he used to crouch over the bat a little bit, he would get too square on sometimes and he was not very happy against the short ball.

Graham will tell you himself that the turning-point came in 1979 when he adopted that unorthodox, upright stance with the bat held in the air which causes such offence to so many old players and coaches. I do not know where he got it from but Tony Greig was the first to use it, Mike Brearley took it up and I think it was from talking to them and possibly Ken Barrington as well about the need to keep his head straight and his eyes level.

Apart from any other consideration, Graham uses a heavy bat, and with a heavy bat you have to have it ready at the top of its arc as the ball is delivered. You just cannot pick it up at the last moment like you can with a lighter bat – although Graham does go to great lengths to make sure that his bats pick up very well anyway, whatever the weight of them. They are not just railway sleepers.

That is typical of the man, too. Everything – bat, gloves, pads, helmet, even that familiar floppy sun hat – have to be just right for him. I think it is something he learned from Keith Fletcher, who was always telling his players: "They are the tools of your trade. If you don't look after them, you cannot do the job properly." But just as Graham adopted the upright stance and then picked up his bat higher than anyone else so he is far more meticulous about his kit than anyone else.

Take his gloves, for example. I have seen players like David Steele, top-class batsman that he was, coming out to bat with holes in the palms of his gloves and the thumbs hanging on by threads. But that would never have done for Fletch, who insisted on having immaculate, clean, dry gloves, and it would never do for Goochy, either.

He goes so far as to having *four* pairs of gloves in his cricket bag, carefully numbered "G.A.G. . . . 1 to 4". He has a superstition about calling for a fresh, right-handed glove whenever he gets to fifty. And he will always start a new session with a clean, dry pair. Sometimes I have picked up the discarded set in the changing-room and thought to myself: "There's nothing wrong with these . . . I'd bat in them." But to Graham they are wet and soiled.

At one stage, he used to sew the top knuckles of his gloves together to make sure they could not be pushed apart as a precaution against having a finger broken. And he was just as fastidious about his pads, stuffing extra bits of padding inside them for increased protection and fiddling around with the straps to make sure that they were just right for him. And he was not content just to make temporary alterations, either. He would go back to the manufacturers whose products were carrying his name with suggested improvements which would benefit other players at every level.

Graham was the first batsman in my experience to have a velcro strip fitted to the inside of his thigh-pad so that he could attach a piece of flannel to soak up the sweat when he batted a long time. Then he could just rip it off and wash it. Ninety per cent of county batsman would just leave their sweat-soaked thigh-pad out in the sun to dry and you can imagine the state they were in by the end of the season. Graham thought that was unhygienic so he invented his own solution which Allan Border, for one, was quick to copy and take back to Australia.

Such meticulous attention to detail shows how much he has thought about every aspect of his game – and it does not just apply to his batting. When he joined Essex he was a batsman who kept wicket – in fact he went on an

England Young Cricketers' tour of the West Indies as number two keeper to Gloucestershire's Andy Stovold – but he soon turned his attention to bowling. If he could be an asset to the side by containing batsmen in one-day cricket by bowling just short of a length around leg stump then that was what he would do – and he did. Not satisfied with that, he learned to swing the ball both ways and he did that so well that in one game against Worcester at Ilford he took seven for fourteen.

I did not play in that match because of an injury and when he came off the field, I said to him: "Well done – but they were my wickets, really, with the ball swinging around like that!"

But that was absolute rubbish. He had made himself into an extremely useful bowler and he deserved full credit for it.

The same goes for his fielding. I think that anybody seeing him in the flesh, as it were, for the first time must be astonished by his reactions and speed off the mark. Television tends to distort the real picture and he can appear muscle-bound and lumbering, but when he springs into action and chases the ball he is quicker than anybody else in our side.

The most remarkable thing about all this – apart from the fact that he has worked out his whole game for himself without ever having to be told to do this or do that – is the level of fitness that has made it possible for him to do it. Just to look at him, he seems to be a terrible shape for a professional sportsman with his heavy frame, bad posture, knock knees and flat feet. Yet, despite his appearance, he has always been a well co-ordinated boy who could play football with the best of them – and since he started training with his beloved West Ham he has reached a level of fitness beyond the most athletic of cricketers.

He has been a Hammers fan ever since his dad, Alf,

used to perch him on that orange box on the Upton Park terraces so it was fairly natural that when he wanted to get himself fit for one winter tour he went and asked the manager, John Lyall, if he could train with them. They were only too pleased to have him – and they were even more pleased when they discovered that he could do almost everything they did. Footballers like Trevor Brooking, Frank Lampard and Billy Bonds, who I have known for years, told me that he fitted in really well. He could not just hold his own in the training sessions but also in the practice matches. They used him as a target man at the back post and he was as competitive as anybody when it came to jumping and challenging for the high ball.

As I found as I got older and began to lose the natural zest of youth, you have to work harder and harder to keep fit and again Graham has taken it so much further than anybody else that one D. L. Acfield used to complain that he had become totally obsessed. It is hard to believe that anyone can run half marathons for fun, but I swear that Graham does, and I am not sure that he appreciates that when it comes to pre-season training everybody else is struggling to keep up with him. It's not just the old ones like Keith Fletcher and myself. It is the eighteen-year-olds as well!

So much for Graham's strengths, but what about his weaknesses? Well, strange as it may seem, the most significant may be that very determination to go to extremes – and especially in his determination to be his own man and do whatever he believes is right for him.

An early example of this came in an all-rounders' challenge tournament which they staged at the Oval one year. Graham believed that he had won it as soon as he scored more runs than anyone else had done, but under the rules of the competition it was quite obvious that he had not because he could still have been out and have had

123

to forfeit some of his runs. Yet he remained adamant that he had won and it was only when he reached the pavilion gate and was told by his father to get back out into the middle that he agreed to play on. Immediately he lost his wicket a couple of times and, in having to slog to try and recoup his losses, he got out again and again. His concentration had gone and he had broken it himself by making up his mind that he had won before he actually had. In the end he did not win – yet if he had accepted the rules in the first place I am sure that he would have walked it.

Since then, of course, that stubborn streak has led him into the far deeper and often murkier waters of sporting politics, and while I will always defend his right and my right to play cricket in South Africa or anywhere else that we want to play, I have to admit that I have not always agreed with his decisions. As I have mentioned, I did not think that he should have gone on that "rebel" tour in 1982 because, just as I was convinced that my Test career was over, I firmly believed that he would have been England's next captain. But he had made up his mind that he was doing the right thing and that was the end of it as far as he was concerned.

Throughout those three years that he was banned, my mind kept going back to that telephone call I had from him and his wife, Brenda, saying that he would be going to South Africa after all – and throughout those years I could not help reflecting on what he and England were missing. He never said very much himself, but the rest of us would pick up the newspapers and say: "Look who they're trying now" – particularly in that dreadful season of 1984 when England were being whitewashed by the West Indies and batsmen like Andy Lloyd and Paul Terry were suffering sickening injuries.

Graham would just nod his head knowingly and get on with his own game. Like me, I think, he had got into the rhythm of playing in a highly successful, super confident county side without having to worry about any outside pressures; like me, he was probably determined to show the selectors what they were missing; and, like me, he had the most prolific season of his career, scoring more than 2,500 runs. It was as if he was saying: "I may be out of Test cricket for three years but I'm still England's number one batsman and there is no way you're going to forget. Here's the weight of runs to make sure you don't!"

As soon as the ban was lifted he had to go straight back into the England side, but there was more controversy to come in 1986 when he took such exception to a statement by an Antiguan politician that he had to be talked out of quitting the tour of the West Indies, and still more the following winter when he made himself unavailable for the Australian tour.

At least that had nothing to do with politics but only the fact that Brenda had just given birth to twins and he was loath to be away for so long. Having studied the tour itinerary and found it impossible to set up a base for his family in Australia, as Ian Botham had done one year, he decided that his family had to come before cricket and this inevitably alienated himself from a large section of the game's followers, who took the view: "If you're picked for England then you've got to go."

In fact that has never been the case because many famous cricketers have been quite selective about where they went to represent England and Graham felt that he could afford to turn England down. It would not have been easy for Brenda to cope on her own with the twins, Megan and Sally, as well as another little girl, Hannah, but I am sure she would not have pushed him into his decision. He would have taken it on his own.

Family life is very important to him. When he is travelling around the country with Essex, he just blends in as one of the lads, but when we are at home he is not the type to pop in for a drink at Ilford Cricket Club, for instance, as I often do. We are completely different people in that respect and, rather than risk an ear-bashing about cricket from some hanger-on or even just a chat with some of the people I want to talk to, he would rather be at home opening a bottle of wine with people he likes.

Because he is so shy and introverted in many ways, it came as a shock to many spectators and television viewers when he showed the other side of his character by suddenly launching into a series of hilarious impersonations to enliven the proceedings as a Test match at Headingley was moving towards a draw. He started off with Bob Willis, capturing all the famous mannerisms of his unique fast-bowling style, and moved on to Chris Old, clutching his back in feigned agony as though he had broken down on his run-up, and John Emburey, gently mocking his best friend's waistline as he hoisted his trousers over his belly. Once again it showed his attention to detail but, more than that, it won over the public. Here was someone they had not seen before, Graham Gooch the entertainer, and everywhere we went after that people were calling on him "to do a Bob Willis" and coming up to us and saying: "He's a funny bloke, old Goochy, isn't he?"

It was nice to think that the Essex changing-room had helped to bring him out of his shell, although he had also matured a lot by then and was the obvious choice to succeed Keith Fletcher as captain, which he did in 1986. And things could not have gone better that year. Graham was away for six Test matches and four one-day internationals so Keith still captained the side in about half the games. This arrangement worked so well that when we won the championship and had a picture taken of them both holding the trophy I thought that it summed up the season perfectly.

They had made an equal contribution and I felt that Graham could not have had a better grounding by doing half the job and letting the old master do the other half. He had obviously learned well from Keith and he did not have many problems, either, as a leader or as a tactician. If anything he was a little bit impatient, tending to move the field too much, especially when the spinners came on, instead of giving them time to settle into a rhythm, but that is a very harsh criticism. Patience comes only with experience and we are comparing Graham in his first year as captain with someone who had been at it for more than twenty years.

None of us suspected what was going to happen in 1987. Again Graham could not have made a better start, scoring 171 in our first championship match against Gloucestershire at Bristol, which we won by ten wickets. But he got "pairs" against Warwickshire and the Pakistanis and with the England selectors ignoring him in favour of the batsmen who had served them well in Australia it was not until the MCC Bicentenary match at Lord's that he really returned to form with a century, batting at number three.

By the end of the year he had still made well over 1,000 runs, yet everybody was saying, "What a bad year Goochy's had." And I suppose he had by his standards. He had been through the sort of run of bad form which can happen to anybody, but it surprised me and a lot of other experienced players that a batsman of his class could get into such a trough.

It just goes to show how much the game is played in the mind because, technique-wise, he had not changed at all. It got to the stage where his confidence had gone to such an extent that he hardly looked like scoring a run and as he grew more and more concerned about his own game form so his leadership suffered and Essex lost direction as a side.

Obviously there were a few moans about it in the changing-room as we failed to make any show in the cup competitions and slipped to twelfth in the championship and fourteenth in the Sunday League, our worst performance for years. But I think we all felt that we could not expect Keith Fletcher to keep coming back and that we had to give Graham a chance. After all, Fletch himself had not started off all that well and we were confident that once Goochy got into better nick with the bat he would be able to give the side a lot more thought.

But it had got him down even more than any of us imagined and to the surprise of everybody – and I do mean everybody – he gave away the captaincy at the end of the season. It was certainly a great shock to me and I was very disappointed in him because I thought that he should have stuck with it and fought his way through it. I was also disappointed that he had not talked to any of the players before making his decision.

The only people who knew about it were Keith Fletcher and Doug Insole, the chairman, and I know that some of the senior players would like to have felt that he could have found it in himself to talk to them about it. He did not say a word until he came to us the following year and explained: "I just couldn't go on. It was making me unhappy." Yet I think we could have talked him out of it if we had had the chance to tell him: "Things don't always run smoothly. You've just got to hang in there."

As things turned out, Graham began to slip back into the captaincy again in 1988 when Keith Fletcher decided that if he played then Nasser Hussain could not, and so stepped down from a number of games to make room for the youngster. And, purely from an Essex point of view, I thought that it was a great shame that we did not win those two closely contested matches against Glamorgan and Nottinghamshire at Colchester which would have given us the championship.

If we had won them, Graham would have had his hands on the trophy for the second time in three years, laid the ghost of Fletcher and put all the trauma of 1987 well behind him. Instead, although he had done everything right and was unlucky not to win both games, there were still some members saying: "If only Fletcher had been in charge, we might have won." It was totally unfounded and very unfair – and Fletch was the first to say so.

All of which left Essex in a real dilemma when Keith finally decided to retire as a player at the end of the 1988 season. Graham had recovered his taste for the job and was ready to accept it again – but, by then, he was captain of England, albeit a captain-in-waiting after the tour to India had been called off. And I for one do not believe that it is possible to combine the jobs of captaining a county and captaining England successfully.

Only time will tell whether the cricket committee came up with the right solution when they reappointed Graham to the county captaincy with Derek Pringle as his vice-captain, which at least gave him, too, the chance to learn the skills of leadership by taking charge for half of the season – assuming that Graham kept the England job as well.

Paradoxically, Graham might have got the England captaincy a bit earlier if he had not been so quick to resign from the position with Essex. For that could well have been taken into consideration when the selectors started looking for a successor to the unfortunate Mike Gatting and came up with those four captains in one series – and five if you want to count Derek Pringle, who deputised when Gooch dislocated a finger at the Oval.

As I have said, any one of them could probably have done the job adequately if the selectors had been prepared to give them more time, but I do not think they gave it enough thought in the first place. John Emburey, for instance, was their first choice for the second Test at Old Trafford when they knew that the third one was being played at Headingley, where they were only going to need one spinner and he was not going to get into the side. Then to replace Emburey with Chris Cowdrey was really clutching at straws. Chris has led Kent very well, but the selectors were looking for the sort of miracle which just does not happen in cricket if they thought that he was going to change the situation against the West Indies. You simply have to pick your best players just to have a chance of competing with them.

Only when that experiment quickly fizzled out through injury did they finally turn to Gooch, who should have been given the job in the first place. Again I go back to the Australian system of giving it to the player who is good enough to be certain of his place in the side – and Graham was the only one who played in all five Tests against the West Indies.

Unfortunately the selectors did not even seem to get that appointment right through what I thought was a lack of foresight. No sooner had Graham taken over than there was all sorts of speculation about whether he would go to India or go back to play in South Africa, where he was believed to have an agreement with Western Province. By the time that had all been cleared up the Indian tour was doomed. Perhaps if the selectors, who must have made up their minds before then, had come straight out with the announcement and stopped the speculation such a sad outcome might have been averted.

But then that was fairly typical of the career of Graham Gooch: the shy, stubborn, single-minded family man who will always have his toolmaking to fall back on.

11

The Border Effect

At the end of the 1985 season, Keith Fletcher called the Essex players together to make an important announcement. "We have been lucky enough," he said, "to have signed Allan Border to play for us next year. As you know, he is a world-class player and if any of you don't learn something from him while he's with us, you need your backsides kicking."

We knew he was a world-class player all right. After all, he was captain of Australia, he was captain of Queensland, he was the third highest scorer in Australian Test history and he had played in more one-day internationals than any other cricketer in the world. What we did not know was how easy he was going to make it for everybody to avoid having their backsides kicked.

I already knew him quite well from playing against him and sharing a few beers with him on my trips to Australia, yet even I was astonished by his attitude to playing county cricket every day of the week. That is all he wanted to do from the day he arrived at Chelmsford and he simply made it impossible for anybody not to learn from him.

It would have been an education in itself just to be able

131

to watch him play, but he had so much more to offer than merely demonstrating his technique. He never came into the changing-room in a morning and said: "Aw, good, it looks like rain ... we could be in for a day off." He just wanted to get out there in the middle and play – and he was not averse to turning out for the 2nd XI, either, if they were one or two players short and the first team did not have a match.

Just how great an influence such a wonderfully re-freshing approach from a cricketer of Allan Border's stature can have on young players in particular is often overlooked by those people, some of them quite influen-tial people, who blame overseas players for the decline in England's Test performances in recent years.

I believe that, in most cases, they have added to our game rather than detracted from it – and that is not to mention the pleasure they have given to the spectators who would have missed so much if all the great players from Sir Garfield Sobers, one of the first arrivals in the Sixties, to Graeme Hick, who emerged from Zimbabwe to become the sensation of the Eighties, had not been allowed to play in English cricket.

The only problem, to my mind, is in getting the balance right, which I think we are close to doing by restricting the number of overseas players to one per county, and closing the qualification loopholes which have enabled some clubs to abuse the system.

In the early days, when counties were allowed to play two each and probably had another one or two in their second teams, it was fair to say that we were bringing along the rest of the world's young cricketers at the expense of our own. (Ironically, South Africa would have been the greatest beneficiaries from that since it was very attractive for counties to sign players who were never going to be lost to Test cricket.)

It is also fair to say that the main reason for reducing

the number from two per county to one is that most clubs would continue to go for two overseas fast bowlers, a policy which has obviously contributed to the shortage of fast bowlers of our own.

As for the abuses, I think it is totally wrong for counties to be able to have two overseas players, invariably fast bowlers, on their staffs even though they are allowed to play only one at a time and simply rotate them so that one of them is always fit and fresh and raring to go. It must be against the spirit of the game if English players are having to perform day in and day out while overseas players are getting a full season's pay for half a season's work.

I am equally sure that every English county cricketer is opposed to the way some clubs have tried to find ways round the regulations concerning qualification – even to the extent of having overseas players classified as English and therefore eligible to play for England when it is transparently obvious that they are not.

There was a good case for reducing Graeme Hick's qualification period from ten years to seven – as the Test and County Cricket Board registration committee did – on the grounds that it was a bit too severe to make a player from a non Test-playing country like Zimbabwe wait from the age of eighteen to twenty-eight before he was eligible to play Test cricket. The fact that he was prepared to wait even seven years was proof enough that he really did want to play for England – especially when he could have got into Test cricket a lot quicker with New Zealand.

But that relaxation of the regulations did produce an anomaly in that it automatically allowed Warwickshire to register Alvin Kallicharran – who had already played in sixty-six Test matches for the West Indies – as an English player and, therefore, technically eligible to play for England. As far as I was concerned, that just did not make sense. I have nothing against Kalli personally and have always found him to be charming, but, if he is never going to be picked for England, how can he possibly be considered English in our domestic competition?

A proposal by the Test and County Cricket Board's Registration and Executive committees to have Hick's qualification period further reduced to only four years, which would have made him eligible to play against Australia in 1990, inevitably got a sympathetic response from everyone who wants to see such a high-class player installed in the England team as soon as possible. But I thought that it could have been setting an even more dangerous precedent and was pleased when a majority of counties endorsed the Cricketers' Association's view that there should be no change from the decision they had made only twelve months earlier.

In fact I believe I speak for the majority of English professionals when I say that I would like to see the regulation clarified once and for all. If a player from overseas wants to spend seven years qualifying to play for England, then he should be allowed to do so. But, if he has played for another country, he should never be classified as English.

This rule would still be fairly lenient in comparison with some other countries. We are not allowed to play in the West Indies' domestic competition, we are not exactly welcomed in Australia, and even South Africa have cut down their overseas players from two per side to one. But, although there are some hard-liners who would like to see us kick out overseas players altogether, I still think they are good for our game.

I am not talking about ordinary players who are no better than those we have already, but about the special ones with something to offer not only to our spectators but also to our playing staffs – and, through them, to English cricket. You have only to look at the contributions some of them have made over the years to know the kind of players I mean.

Where would Nottinghamshire be today without the revitalising effect of first Garry Sobers and, more recently, Clive Rice and Richard Hadlee? Would Lancashire have won all those one-day trophies without the addition of the supreme talent of Clive Lloyd to an already talented side? Could Gloucestershire have become a county to be feared if Mike Procter had not instilled such a fighting spirit in the days when we called them "Proctershire"? Would Derbyshire have even survived without Eddie Barlow, the inspiration of their present captain, Kim Barnett?

In comparison with them, the impact of Allan Border on Essex may seem minimal. But I can assure you that every single one of us learned something from him – and our youngsters, especially, should be eternally grateful if any aspect of his approach to the game rubbed off on them.

I do not know how he came to play for us in the first place, but it was certainly quite a coup by whoever was responsible. I know it was not because we were paying him a huge amount of money, as many people seemed to imagine, so I think it could only have been because he wanted to play for us, which is always the best way to recruit anybody.

He rapidly became one of the boys – nicknamed "Herbaceous" for obvious reasons – and, although he was only with us for one season initially and had to leave a month before the end of that to captain Australia in India, he was as committed as anybody. And that commitment was never more apparent than when the conditions were at their worst.

One such occasion was against Middlesex at Lord's where the pitch was so green and treacherous that twenty-eight wickets fell by lunch on the second day before we were eventually left to get 176 to win. Wayne Daniel and Norman Cowans were frightening, breaking Keith Fletcher's finger and hitting just about everybody else, but "A.B.", batting without a helmet and simply swaying out of the way of the most lethal deliveries, saw us to victory by five wickets.

I can still remember it well even though I was actually playing for England at the time and had other things on my mind because, when I met up with the lads again, they were still on a high after winning a match that they thought they had no chance of winning and just could not stop talking about Allan's performance.

He continued to show that sort of commitment even after he had left us, keeping in touch by telephone and telegram throughout the tense, closing weeks of that 1986 season until we finally clinched the championship in our last match but one at Trent Bridge. If anything, he showed even more when, quite unexpectedly, he came back to play for us again in 1988.

I suppose it was some kind of comment on the deterioration of English pitches that this was the season in which "A.B." acquired the further nickname of "Van Gogh" and decided it was time that he started wearing a helmet to bat in.

It is no macho thing not to wear a helmet. It is just that some players like Allan Border and Viv Richards have so much confidence in their ability – and some like Richie Richardson of the West Indies so little experience of English conditions – that they do not feel the need to wear one. But there are so many fast bowlers and so many bad pitches around these days that, no matter how good you are, somebody is going to catch up with you sooner or later.

Allan's time came against Warwickshire at Edgbaston where Tony Merrick struck him on the side of the head with such force that he needed twenty stitches on the outside of his ear and another ten inside it, which is obviously where "Van Gogh" came from. And it made me cringe to see him easing a borrowed helmet – he did not even have one of his own – over his blood-soaked ear before going out to do battle again.

In circumstances like that, he is just about the best player in the world today and he provided an object lesson in how to bat on such a bad pitch that even he came in at lunchtime and said: "I can't see how I'm going to get a run out there." But, having refused to give his wicket away by battling away throughout a whole session, he went out after lunch and smashed the ball around to finish up with 112.

It was not enough to save us in that particular match – Warwickshire somehow confounded everything that had gone before by winning by five wickets – but it left a deep impression on everyone who saw it. Personal pride came into it, of course, because he just could not tolerate losing his wicket to bowlers he did not rate too highly and could only cause him problems because of the state of the pitch. But, on top of that, he combined ability, courage and commitment in a way that was wonderful to see.

Incidentally, "A.B." did get himself a helmet of his own after that experience. He had gone around the changing-room looking for one that was comfortable and finally settled on a helmet without a chin-strap – only to find that it leapt off his head when he ducked a bouncer. His reflexes were sharp enough for him to catch it one-handed as it came down but, when he got back, he said: "It's no good. This is stupid. I'm going to have to get one."

We also had the benefit of his experience as a captain that year – although, with respect to people like Mike Procter and Clive Rice who have been such inspiring leaders, I must say that I do not like to see counties being captained by overseas players. I am very much in favour of English players doing the job because it takes a long time to learn the art of captaincy, but if we are going to give the job to overseas players we are never going to find good captains of our own.

To be fair to Allan, he did not really want to captain Essex, arguing that he had only joined us to play his cricket. But, with Keith Fletcher and Brian Hardie injured, Graham Gooch and Derek Pringle with England and the only other senior player – me! – not having the best of track records as captain, he agreed to take on the job.

My only previous experience of captaincy had been in similar circumstances and ended in defeat inside two days! Allan was to prove more successful, putting Yorkshire in on a helpful pitch and winning fairly comfortably in the end – but not before I had bowled unchanged throughout the first session, a little matter of two-and-a-quarter hours.

He kept coming up to me and saying: "Are you all right?" And I kept telling him: "Yes, I'm fine." But, when we got back to the pavilion at lunchtime, Keith Fletcher was waiting to have a go at him.

"Look here," said Fletch, with touching concern for my state of health, "he's nearly forty, you know. You can't do that to him."

"Naw, he's all right," replied A.B. "You're all right, J.K., aren't you?"

"Yes, I'm fine," I gasped for the umpteenth time that morning.

"Well . . . maybe," said Fletch doubtfully. "But you go and get your lunch and I'll stay here and see if he wants any oxygen."

All that was forgotten, naturally, when we won the game thanks to Neil Foster's ten wickets in the match – and you could see how much it meant to Allan that the decisions he had made had been the right ones and brought about the desired result.

He had to leave before the end of that season, too – this time to captain Australia in Pakistan. But, even though he walked straight into the same kind of problems that Mike Gatting had faced there the year before, he still found time to get through on the phone and wish us well during our championship run-in.

"We've just had twenty-five shouts for LBW and not one of them's been given out yet," he said one day. "How are you doing?"

Unfortunately we were not doing quite well enough and eventually finished third behind Worcestershire and Kent – but that was not Allan Border's fault. He has been a tremendous asset to Essex, giving our membership, which he swelled by at least a thousand, the chance to see one of the best batsmen in the world in every home game and, perhaps more importantly in the long term, having an incalculable effect on our younger players.

12

A Shock Recall

The England selectors have given me a few surprises over the years but nothing quite like the shock I got in June 1986, when they picked me for the second Test against India at Headingley. I was thirty-seven years old, I had not played Test cricket for more than four years and, at the time, I did not think that I was bowling particularly well.

I do not really know why I felt like that. Everything had gone right for me in the first seven matches of the season, which had produced thirty-one wickets, including five for thirty-two against Derbyshire and six for fifty-seven against Glamorgan. But, for some unknown reason, I was not happy with my performances in the next two games against Nottinghamshire at Chelmsford and Hampshire at Ilford, when I picked up only four wickets at a total cost of 230 runs.

It was only a question of confidence. I had no injuries or any other problems and, although it did not cross my mind at the time, I wondered afterwards whether it might have had anything to do with all the speculation about the selectors looking at me again with a view to recalling me at Headingley. At first I ridiculed the idea, thinking it was no more than the Essex jokers winding me up. But, as it began to seem more realistic, perhaps I panicked a bit. As I say, I do not know.

I could not fault the selectors' thinking. England had just lost the first Test of the three-match series at Lord's by five wickets – their sixth defeat in a row – and by the time it was over they had sacked David Gower as captain and replaced him with Mike Gatting. Obviously they wanted to try to level the series at Leeds on what was bound to be "a result pitch" which gave them their best chance against the powerful Indian batting line-up.

In that respect it was very much a one-off situation – as I would have explained to any younger bowlers who might, quite understandably, have thought: "If they're going to bring back a thirty-seven-year-old, what hope is there for us?" I could certainly feel for them, but the point was that Headingley is notorious for being a place where the ball swings as well as seams and I could not see anything wrong with the "horses for courses" theory.

The crucial question was: "Had they backed the right horse?" They had several bowlers injured, including a swing specialist, Richard Ellison, who was in the squad but never likely to play, so I knew that I was not the first choice. And I must admit that I felt more nervous going in to that Test than I had ever felt before – even on my England debut in Delhi. I had no great track record at Headingley – indeed most of my games for Essex against Yorkshire had been played on other grounds like Scarborough and Sheffield – and it was a very strange feeling indeed.

I felt even stranger when Laurie Brown, the team's physiotherapist, took the players out for the warm-up which has become very much a part of the pre-match preparation these days. Fred Titmus, one of the selectors, was standing by the pavilion steps as I went past and he said: "Look, you take it easy out there. You're no chicken, you know. You just do what you normally do and don't go running around like the rest of them. We don't want you getting knackered before we even start."

"All right, Fred," I said. "I'll be careful."

Obviously he had visions of me doing three or four laps and then collapsing in a heap, which I thought was a bit much coming from somebody who had played first-class cricket until he was fifty – and with four toes missing at that! But, seriously, he did help me and put me more at ease because I felt that the selectors appreciated what they were asking me to do and what I might be going through.

There was one other problem, though, which did nothing to boost my confidence. On the few occasions when I had played at Headingley before, I had always run up the hill from the Football Stand End – just as I had always run up the hill at Chelmsford or Ilford or wherever else I played. When I first started, Keith Boyce always liked to run down the hill with the wind behind him and I had no choice other than to get used to bowling from the other end. But on that particular day at Leeds the wind was in the wrong direction for me. A stiff breeze was blowing across the ground from the players' pavilion, which meant that I would have to run down the hill from the Kirkstall Lane End if it was going to help my inswing. That gave me a mental block even before India's captain, Kapil Dev, won the toss and chose to bat.

I had never bowled that well running down a slope. If it is not too bad you can get away with it, but at Headingley it is so steep that there is always a feeling that you will topple too far forward in your action and tend to overpitch – all of which was going through my mind and making me more nervous than ever.

The upshot was that I conceded eighteen runs in my first two overs and thirty-one in my first seven without taking a wicket, and at the end of that opening spell I said to Mike Gatting: "I wouldn't mind having a go at the other end." But the breeze was quite strong and it would have been very hard for me to have bowled into it so we decided against a switch.

Derek Pringle, replacement for the suspended Ian Botham, eventually got us into the game with the wickets of Srikkanth and Gavaskar, but Vengsarkar and Pandit had taken India past 200 by the time I made any impression by dismissing Vengsarkar and Kapil Dev with successive balls. And my final figures of two for 102 in thirty overs could not have been what the selectors had in mind when they picked me.

As we were to learn from bitter experience, it is best to bat first at Headingley when the pitch is damp because, as it dries out, the bounce becomes more variable. But, at the time, we were not too sure what was going to happen and felt that their total of 272 was not beyond our capabilities. We were wrong.

From the moment that Graham Gooch played half back to Kapil Dev and the ball hit the corner of his bat and flew to gully, we knew that we were in trouble. It was not the kind of dismissal that you would expect from a bowler of Kapil's pace and it put so many doubts in the minds of the other batsmen that we batted really badly and were all out for 102 in next to no time.

To be fair to the Indian bowlers, I must confess that they did the job I was supposed to do rather better than I did. It was simply a matter of pitching the ball on the right line and length, swinging it a fraction and waiting for the pitch to do the rest. Madan Lal, recalled, like me, at the age of thirty-five from the Central Lancashire League specifically to exploit such conditions, and Roger Binny did it superbly.

At least I felt more relaxed at the start of their second innings. There was somebody in the crowd who I could hear shouting: "Come on, J.K. – just imagine you're bowling for Essex!" And Graham Gooch, who, I suspect, could sense the tension inside me, kept running up from slip at the end of each over to give me a few words of advice and encouragement and a reassuring pat on the backside.

Both of my Essex supporters helped me a lot and I felt that my luck had changed when I had the master – Gavaskar – brilliantly caught behind down the legside by Bruce French, who was making his Test debut. It is always an unlucky way for a batsman to get out and especially at Headingley, because any slight deflection can easily race away for four down that slope.

I was still bowling down the hill but two LBW decisions against Shastri and Azharuddin gave me three wickets in twenty-eight balls and suddenly things were starting to click. We had them on the run at seventy for five by the end of the second day, and if we could have got one more wicket early on Saturday morning I think we might still have got a different result. After all, you only have to bowl a side out cheaply once to give yourselves a chance of winning.

But it was not to be. It took us a long time to get rid of the night watchman, More, and we could not get rid of Vengsarkar at all. Having bowled thirty overs in the first innings and not had too much rest before starting all over again, I had run out of steam and we were really up against it as Vengsarkar went on to complete an un-beaten century and leave us to get 408 to win.

It was impossible, of course, Kapil Dev and Binny accounted for Graham Gooch and Wilf Slack and then the Indian spinners came into their own – so much so that just before the close I found myself going in to bat as night watchman. I pushed forward to my first ball from Maninder Singh which must have turned because I got a faint nick to the wicketkeeper. And even now I can see the look on umpire Jack Birkenshaw's face as I just stood there quite unable to believe what had happened.

I do not know why I waited until his finger went up because I am a walker and I always go when I hit it without even bothering to look at the umpire. I was going that time as well, but I just could not help staring at him as I thought to myself: "Crikey! That's turned and I've hit it." I was still in a state of shock when I got back to the changing-room.

The contrast between my first Test and what I was now convinced would be my last had been remarkable. At Delhi I had gone in as night watchman and made fifty-three. Now I had gone in as night watchman and got out first ball which, again, was not quite doing the job that I was supposed to do.

So by Saturday night I had bowled twice and I had batted twice and there was only one thing for it – to get myself down to the local pub and have a few pints of Tetleys, which I did. Sunday was a recovery period. And so was Monday after we had lost our four remaining wickets by 12.15 and been beaten by 279 runs.

I was bitterly disappointed. I was going away with six wickets but I knew I could – and should – have bowled a lot better than I did and I was under no illusions about my England future. So I was a little bit surprised that when we went our separate ways, Mike Gatting said: "See you at the next Test at Edgbaston."

"That can't be right, surely," I thought to myself. And it was not. My Test career was over.

13

England Crisis

It was no more than a coincidence, of course, but following my last appearance for England we won only two of our next twenty-six Test matches before stopping the rot against Sri Lanka at Lord's more than two years later. Those two wins were enough for us to retain the Ashes in Australia in 1986–87 but then we went for eighteen Tests against Australia (two), Pakistan (eight), New Zealand (three) and the West Indies (five) without a single victory, drawing eleven of those matches and losing seven.

Such an unprecedented run of failure was hardly a convincing argument in favour of the appointment of England's first full-time team manager – Mickey Stewart, the former Surrey batsman, captain and manager – who took over on an experimental basis on that successful Australian tour and was rewarded with a three-year contract. But, personally, I do not think that what has happened since is his fault. In fact I believe that the appointment of an individual with complete control of the side, including selection, is the best answer to the crisis facing English cricket – although I would not give him the title of "manager". It has always been and always will be the captain's job to run the side on the field and he has got to be the number one. The term "manager" conjures up too many images of football and people who seem to be bigger than their clubs and even the game itself, and I would hate to see cricket becoming associated with anything like that.

"Administrator", "director" or even just "selector" might be a better name for the job I have in mind, some aspects of which I have already observed at very close quarters. Take, for example, Keith Fletcher's role when he has not been playing for Essex for one reason or another, Graham Gooch has taken over the captaincy and, without detracting in any way from his authority, Fletcher has always been there to advise him on team selection and tactics, to motivate others and to enhance the side's performance in whatever way he could.

In a similar vein, I played most of my Test cricket on tour when the late Kenny Barrington was either manager or assistant manager and he was another tremendous influence. When you came off the field after making runs or taking wickets and saw that beaming face in the changing-room it was magic, it really was. Conversely, if a batsman got himself out to a poor shot, his first reaction would be: "What will Kenny say?"

He really could get through to the players in that way and it did not matter who they were or how they thought about the game. You have only got to talk to such contrasting characters as Mike Brearley and Derek Randall and they will say exactly the same kind of things about the effect he had on them.

When Kenny died so tragically in the West Indies in 1981, I felt that England needed someone like him to take his place and I think that they have probably found such a man in Mickey Stewart. He is out of the same mould and will think nothing about spending hour after hour in the nets just throwing the ball down to help a player to get things right. And I think that he has done quite a good job – insofar as he has been allowed to do it.

The drawback is that he is still in the hands of his fellow-selectors – and particularly the chairman – and there, I feel, is where much of the problem lies. Great players as they unquestionably were and well meaning as they undoubtedly are, I cannot believe that men like Alec Bedser, who held the job for thirteen years, and Peter May, who did it for the next seven, can possibly understand what is going on out in the middle these days. I find it hard enough to comprehend all the changes that have taken place in the years that I have been playing, so people like Alec Bedser, who retired in 1960 and went into business, or Peter May, who left the game in 1963 to work in the City, must have been at a huge disadvantage.

I know that Mickey Stewart has not actually played the game for a long time, either, but he has kept in touch through his work with the Surrey and England players – and also through his own son, Alec, who, as one of the most promising young batsmen in the country, knows the difficulties facing the modern cricketer only too well.

As an employee of the Test and County Cricket Board, he is also in a position to watch a lot more cricket than the unpaid selectors, who just go and see what games they can – and, more often than not, only at Lord's or another of the bigger grounds. Players at the more unfashionable counties often complain that they only see the selectors once or twice a season and that even when they do turn up they get the feeling that they have come to see the opposition rather than them.

We at Essex are probably luckier in that respect since the most obvious change in the game from my point of view has been our transformation from a hard-up, middle-of-the-table club into an attractive, relatively well-off county, consistently capable of challenging for the major prizes. But success has brought its own pressures and probably made us more aware than most of the fundamental changes in the way the game is played throughout the country and how they are affecting the development of players.

There is no shortage of talent in English cricket. On the contrary, there is stacks of talent. It is just a question of harnessing that talent and bringing it along in the right way, and I do not think that we are doing that at the moment.

For a start, there is a lot more money around these days – not so much in the players' pockets, unless they happen to be playing Test cricket regularly, but in the counties' coffers – with the result that there is no longer such a thing as an easy game. The increased revenue from one-day cricket, improved marketing and greater spon-sorship has meant that every side has been able to import at least one proven match-winner and sometimes two, and every side is capable of beating anybody else if their particular match-winner is in form on any particular day.

There is not a first-class county which has not got what the players call "a super quick" – with the possible exception of Yorkshire, although they have a very talented fast bowler of their own in Paul Jarvis – and the very presence of such predators has turned county cricket into a jungle where batsmen could become an en-dangered species.

There is no way, for example, that any county with a promising young opening batsman in the 2nd XI should throw him into the first team as an opener until he has learned to look after himself. What Essex did with Graham Gooch when we started him off down at number seven and gradually pushed him up the order was the right way to do it. And nowadays, I think, it is even more important.

The pitches we play on only add to the dangers. There has certainly been a deterioration in the general standard over the years and that has been compounded by a marked increase in the number of pitches that are deliberately prepared to produce a result.

Bad pitches are great "levellers" – even to the extent that minor counties can beat first-class counties, as we found out to our cost when we lost to Hertfordshire at Hitchin in the Gillette Cup. Yet every minor county that we have met on a decent pitch at Chelmsford has failed to subdue our batsmen and then struggled to get anywhere near the required run-rate themselves.

"Result pitches" seem to have become all-important to some counties in the championship, but it is a short-sighted policy which is bound to backfire on England. We are not only going to be short of batsmen but we are going to be short of bowlers, too, because they will have no idea how to bowl on flat pitches when they get into Test cricket.

I was against the introduction of four-day cricket in the championship, but if that and the appointment of a new pitches' supremo – Harry Brind, who learned his craft at Chelmsford before going to to do such a fine job at the Oval – combine to produce better pitches and consequently better batsmen and better bowlers then it will be all to the good.

Apart from the players of exceptional ability like Graham Gooch, David Gower, Mike Gatting, Allan Lamb and, of course, the prolific Graeme Hick, there are many good batsmen in county cricket, batsmen who are very hard to shift once they get in and who are always going to get their runs because they will never whack the ball up in the air to give you an easy wicket.

They are the solid, reliable, above all experienced county players – Mark Benson and Neil Taylor at Kent, Chris Tavare (now with Somerset), Chris Broad and Tim Robinson at Nottinghamshire, Bill Athey at Gloucestershire, the late Wilf Slack at Middlesex, Martyn Moxon at

Yorkshire and Chris Smith at Hampshire are some of the names that spring to mind. They see too many bad pitches not to make sure that they cash in when they get on to a good one. As you run up to bowl at them, you can actually sense the way they are thinking: "This is a nice, flat pitch . . . I'm not going to take a chance here."

This is the attitude of mind that the younger, often more gifted players have still to learn and it is not easy for them to do it on some of the pitches they have to play on. When the ball is moving around all over the place, they can hang in there for an hour and still get out for ten so they tend to think that they may as well play a few shots and get out for thirty or forty, which could be a match-winning score anyway. If they played on better pitches, they might be more prepared to spend an hour making ten or twenty in the knowledge that batting was going to get easier the longer they stayed in and that and the runs would come eventually – as Allan Border demonstrated in that memorable innings at Edgbaston.

Life is more difficult for the modern bowlers, too, not so much because of the pitches, obviously, although, as I have said, bad pitches do have an adverse effect when bowlers play on a Test pitch, but more because of the influence of one-day cricket.

Where this is most apparent is in the desperate shortage of young spinners who are simply not getting the chance to learn to bowl the right way in the longer, first-class game before having to adjust to the limited-overs version with its emphasis on runs per over rather than runs per wicket. Instead of learning to bowl properly with fielders in the right attacking positions, they have to bowl to defensive fields, spearing the ball in around leg stump, and it does them no good at all.

We have produced some of the better slow bowlers in one-day cricket, men like Derek Underwood, Ray East, Norman Gifford, John Emburey, Eddie Hemmings and

Jack Simmons, who could make it virtually impossible to score a run at times, but they all learned to bowl the right way in three-day cricket and were good enough to adapt to the shorter game and back again. Today's youngsters are being thrown in at the deep end and many of them sink before they can swim.

Yet spinners are not the only ones who are suffering. I firmly believe that one of the reasons why our quicker bowlers seem to pick up so many more injuries is because of the intense pressure and sheer physical demands of the one-day game.

They may have to bowl only eight, eleven or twelve overs in the match but they are not expected to bowl one bad ball in those spells. And, apart from all the concentration involved in that, they also have to do their share of the fielding and throw themselves all over the place to stop that single run which might just be the difference between winning and losing. I am sure the amount of one-day cricket is taking its toll of our bowlers and making it increasingly hard for them to stay fit.

Another reason, incidentally, which has nothing to do with one-day cricket but has been a particular bone of contention of mine over the years, is that our bowlers have not been properly equipped to go abroad during the winter and play on pitches which are so much harder than the ones we play on at home.

It is only in the past couple of years or so that we have managed to get cricket boot manufacturers to sit down with us and try to do something about this particular problem. Whereas batsmen have always been able to advertise the make of bat they were using, bowlers in English cricket have had to wear plain white boots so there was no incentive for the manufacturers to become involved.

We just had to make do with a basic pair of boots and then fiddle around with them ourselves, slipping in inner

15. A part of cricketing contact with South Africa which
the politicians choose to ignore. My friend and sponsor,
Ernie Du Plessis, with some of the sports equipment we collected
and distributed among black schoolchildren in 1985.

16. Seam-up against Northamptonshire's Allan Lamb at
Colchester under the watchful eyes of non-striker Rob Bailey and
umpire David Lloyd.

17/18. Lever the batsman – (above) giving it the block against Leicestershire's Ken Higgs but (below) on the charge against some unsuspecting Glamorgan spinner. Roger Tolchard and Eifion Jones are the wicketkeepers.

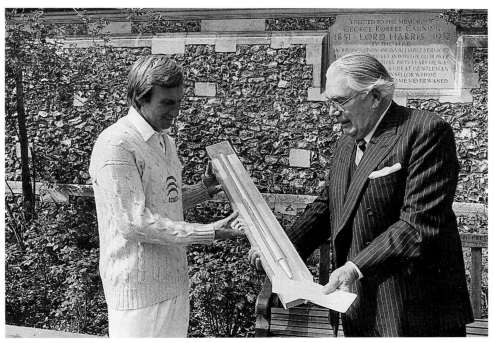

19/20. Symbols of success. (Above) E. W. Swanton, legendary
Daily Telegraph cricket correspondent, presents me with a silver
stump for being the first bowler to take 100 wickets in 1983 while
(below) statistician Andy Trimnell marks my record 350 wickets
in the Sunday League. (*Top, Daily Telegraph*)

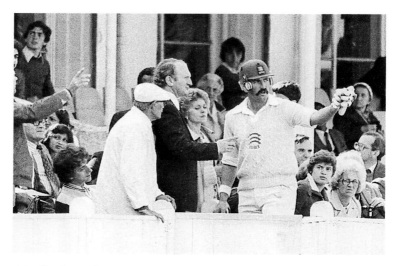

21. Graham Gooch reveals his single-mindedness. With his wife, Brenda, by his side, he is arguing that he has won a single-wicket competition at the Oval in 1979. In fact, he lost.

22. Allan Border, complete with helmet and chin-strap which he only felt the need to wear after he joined Essex and encountered some of the pitches we have to play on.

soles to cushion the impact, putting padding in the heels to prevent chafing and suchlike. You name it, we have tried it. Now, at last, the TCCB has allowed the manufacturers to put a distinctive flash on their footwear and, now that there is something in it for them, some companies are working really hard to produce decent bowling boots.

It may not sound like the most significant development in the history of the game but, believe me, it could make a tremendous difference. As a bowler myself, I believe that if you do not look after your feet, the trouble can work its way up until it affects the knees and the back. The right kind of materials and design could just help to prolong the careers of bowlers like Graham Dilley and Neil Foster, who have had more than their share of these problems.

That would obviously be a great bonus for England since Graham and Neil are now established as our best fast bowlers, which says as much for their characters as it does for their ability. There are others like Greg Thomas who can bowl just as quick and probably quicker, but pace is just the raw ingredient, a basis to work on.

I do not know whether some people think that they have made it just because they can hurl the ball down really fast, but that is only the start of the learning process in a bowling sense. It is not enough just to bowl a few bouncers interspersed by the odd good ball, and Graham and Neil are classic examples of bowlers who have learned – not before playing in quite a few Test matches, mind you – to put the ball in the right spot and do something with it without losing any of their pace.

You also need temperament to go with your ability and that is what I hope Phillip DeFreitas will learn in the not too distant future. "Daffy" is a very talented all-round player, but he has played a lot of cricket for his age and came back from Australia not so long ago looking very tired. And I am not sure that he has yet got the right temperament to turn himself into an all-rounder in the Ian Botham mould.

Temperament is something that you can learn. It does not have to be bred in you; you can learn to turn your back when things are going wrong – or Jonathan Agnew has chucked your kit over the balcony just because you poured salt on his lunch! – and get on with your own game. I think that DeFreitas' move from Leicestershire to Lancashire should help him to do that. He has the ability, now he has to get his temperament sorted out. A new manager like Alan Ormrod, a new captain like David Hughes and a fresh set of lads like Lancashire have could be the making of him. If it is not, there will have to be a big question-mark against him.

In addition to Dilley, Foster and DeFreitas, there are any number of seam bowlers – Gladstone Small, Phil Newport, Derek Pringle, Neal Radford, the aforemen- tioned Jonathan Agnew and the emerging Angus Fraser among them – who have all excelled in English conditions and many people must wonder why we do not even do well in Test matches at home. While I know as well as anybody does that it is a big step from county cricket to Test cricket, I cannot help wondering whether we make the most of our resources.

If anybody asks a county cricketer why he does not spend as much time practising as, say, professional golfers do, he will amost certainly reply: "I'm playing every day . . . I just haven't got time to practise."

That is probably true to a certain extent, but it should not stop cricketers from talking about the game and trying to learn as much as they can. I think that there are a lot of bowlers in county cricket who need to talk to other bowlers even if it is only to boost their confidence and give them belief in themselves. If they have got a specific problem, they should seek advice. They would probably find themselves being told: "Oh, yes, I've had that. It's because you're doing so-and-so."

There is not enough of that kind of thing happening in some county sides. There are some wise, old captains who will tell a young spinner: "Go and see Embers [John Emburey] and have a chat with him." But I believe that many more should take advantage of such a ready access to information.

I do not want to keep harping on about the way we do things at Essex, but we do talk to each other a great deal, batsmen with batsmen, bowlers with bowlers, to try to sort out our mutual problems. And although it might just be a coincidence that we have done well over the years, it might just be one answer to England's problems as well. After all, we do need to pull together because while we have been struggling just to maintain our standards in international cricket, it seems to me that the other Test-playing countries have improved out of all recognition.

Again, I think that money must have had something to do with it. People used to talk of young, black Americans taking up boxing to escape the poverty trap, and I think the same thing probably applies to cricket as far as young West Indians and Pakistanis are concerned. There is a lot of money to be earned at the highest level and they have come on by leaps and bounds in their professionalism to make sure that they obtain their share of it.

If the West Indies have had the best fast bowlers in Test cricket in recent years then Pakistan have had the best batsmen with a succession of world-class players like Majid Khan, Asif Iqbal, Zaheer Abbas, Wasim Raja and Javed Miandad always making sure that they have had enough runs on the board.

With Imran Khan taking wickets as well as scoring runs, they are the only side who have really challenged the supremacy of the West Indies – which is not really too surprising when you consider the strength of their attack. Their bowlers are not only quick but they also know exactly what they are doing, and I am sure that much of the credit for that must go to Andy Roberts.

When he was playing county cricket, first with Hampshire and then with Leicestershire, Andy was for ever thinking and talking about the game. You could mention any batsman he had played against and, with a little smile and a glint in his eye, he would immediately come up with their weakness. He stored all that information and in time passed it on to Michael Holding, Joel Garner, Malcolm Marshall, Courtney Walsh and all the rest of them, including Colin Croft, who had the best strike of them all. All the lads who played against him said that he bowled the last ball of the day as quick as he did the first, and that sort of strength and stamina combined with Andy's supreme bowling intelligence was quite devastating.

New Zealand were another country who began producing cricketers like Richard Hadlee, Geoff Howarth, John Wright, Martin Crowe and one or two more who made our lives a misery. Suddenly the kind of domination that England had known against the supposedly inferior sides for most of the time that the present selectors were playing had gone.

I know that some of them will argue that we did the rest of the world's players a great favour by allowing so many of them into county cricket. But, although I cannot dispute the fact that we have helped every Test-playing country by furthering their players' educations and giving them invaluable experience of English conditions, I have also seen – and already outlined – the benefits that overseas cricketers have brought to us.

While I am on the subject of learning to become a Test cricketer from playing in different conditions, I would like to pay tribute to Derrick Robins for enabling me and many, many more future England players to go abroad on the tours he used to run and suggest that this is another area where our youngsters are not getting the same opportunities as we did. I was fortunate enough to go on two of Derrick's tours, both to South Africa, and was grateful to get the chance to play overseas, which is so different from playing at home.

Derrick Robins, a former chairman of Coventry City Football Club who had played a couple of games for Warwickshire as a wicketkeeper-batsman, was a wonderfully benevolent cricketing sponsor long before anyone had even heard of Cornhill, staging nearly two hundred matches in England, notably at the Saffrons ground at Eastbourne, and taking teams to Australia, Canada, South America and the Orient as well as South Africa.

His tours were so well organised that they were like mini MCC tours, even down to the blazers and sweaters. He would use his games at the Saffrons to select a carefully balanced, essentially harmonious mixture of experienced players and younger ones who could learn from them, and he took great delight when any of them was picked for England in being able to say: "He was one of my boys."

I could never see anything wrong with that because it is something that I would love to do myself if I had the money. He did have a record to be proud of when you consider that Bob Willis, David Gower, Mike Gatting, John Emburey, Phil Edmonds, David Bairstow, Mike Hendrick, Derek Randall, Clive Radley, Graham Roope, Roger Tolchard and Bob Woolmer were just a few of his old boys.

A lot of our younger players today do go abroad to coach and play club cricket, but unless they get the chance to play Sheffield Shield in Australia or Currie Cup in South Africa, which very few of them do, it is nothing like as beneficial as going away for six weeks or so on a

properly organised tour with senior players to help you
and top-class opposition to play against.

Some of our more promising boys who have been to
Australia on Whitbread Scholarships, for example, have
come home saying that it did them more harm than good.
They were playing once a week in club cricket which was
all too easy for them, and a batsman only had to get a bad
decision one Saturday and be rained off the next to find
himself without a decent knock for a month.

Sadly, the days of the cricketing entrepreneurs like
Derrick Robins and one or two more seem to have gone
and, with more and more Test and one-day international
cricket being played, even dates are hard to find. But I am
sure that Micky Stewart must be investigating the
possibility of reintroducing regular England "B" tours –
which are what Derrick was virtually running – to bridge
that gap in our players' education.

In the meantime, it is back to the reality of the present
situation – and I have to return to my original point that
the main reason why England have had such a wretched
run of results in the past couple of years is because the
selectors have not kept up with the changes that have
taken place and consequently lost touch with the modern
game.

Take the most recent series against the West Indies. I
am well aware that there is a huge difference between
one-day internationals and Test matches, but we won all
three of the limited-overs matches at the start of the
summer and we won them so convincingly that there
must have been something there for the selectors to build
on. We even managed to halt a run of ten successive
defeats against the West Indies by drawing the first Test,
which made losing the next four seem quite incredible.

Sacking Mike Gatting did not help. He is not a bad
motivator by any means. He treats his bowlers the right
way and gets people going in the field. The sheer guts of

his batting sets a great example to the rest of the side, and when he was relieved of the captaincy for a reason understood only by the selectors the whole structure that he and Mickey Stewart seemed to have been constructing fell apart.

That decision was sadly typical, I felt, of the inconsistency that can so easily undermine any side. The selectors have only got to get one or two decisions wrong and the entire side is up against it. You need to look no further than the County Championship to see what happens when a team is without one or two key players through injuries or Test calls or whatever. It makes all the difference between winning and losing.

This is another area where they are not in touch with the current thinking in county changing-rooms where we are aghast when people like David Gower and Allan Lamb are sometimes left out. They are not the best of county players – indeed David's position in some county sides would be questioned on his record in the past year or so – but as Test players they are in a different league. It seems to me that some people, including the media, do not understand that when they get on to the Test stage they perform three or four levels higher than they do in the championship.

I think that we have got to start picking balanced sides as well. It is just no good for the selectors to say: "Our batting is dreadfully weak so we've got to pick an extra batsman and leave out a bowler." The fact of the matter is that if you cannot bowl out the other side, you are not going to win a Test match.

Perhaps there is a case for strengthening the batting against the West Indies and looking to draw a game now and then. If you cannot pick a side that you think is going to win then you can be forgiven for picking a side that you think is not going to lose. But, even so, I do not really believe that the selectors go to enough trouble to look at the pitches we are going to be playing on and then make absolutely sure that we start the match with the right line-up.

It would not go down too well with the counties, which naturally do not want to lose any more players than is absolutely necessary, but I think we have got to get our priorities right. And if we really want a successful England team we should perhaps be picking thirteen or fourteen players and then making a final choice on the morning of the match when all the necessary information has been obtained. Let us face it. Touring sides have sixteen players to choose from, so why should we handicap ourselves by selecting from only twelve?

There have been many times when we at Essex have thought that England have gone into a Test match with the wrong seam bowling line-up or the wrong spinning combination simply because the team has been picked in London on a Friday to start a Test match in an altogether different part of the country the following Thursday.

I suppose it does go to show how much we care about England's performances, which might surprise a few people. I did go through a period when I was banned from Test cricket and deliberately concentrated all my thoughts on what Essex were doing, but gone are the days when disgruntled England players let it be known: "I haven't been picked so I hope they get a bloody good hiding."

Even Keith Fletcher, who has probably had more reason than most to feel disenchanted with the England set-up in the past few years, is constantly switching on the radio or television when a Test match is in progress to find out how well we are doing . . . not how badly.

Obviously we want any of our team-mates who might have been picked to do well for themselves, but we want England to do well, too. That is very much a part of the Essex philosophy. Even if we do not always agree with the selectors, we do not want to see England being rolled over by the West Indies or Australia or anybody else.

To me, that would undo all the good that we are trying to do in county cricket, anyway. It is an enormous step-up from there to Test cricket, but we have still got to set certain standards to start with. And if England are not doing well it reflects badly on us and suggests that our standards are not high enough.

14

Hopes And Fears

It hurts me to say so because I cannot envisage a better way of earning a living, but I have to say that if I was a youngster just beginning my cricket career I would be very worried about the future.

For all the changes that have taken place during my time with Essex, the situation for a county cricketer has been comparatively stable and secure when you consider the upheavals that have taken place in other sports and, indeed, in other walks of life. But suddenly everything seems to be decidedly shaky.

Nobody could be quite sure what was going to happen at the end of 1988 as the Test and County Cricket Board prepared to discuss the entire structure of the domestic game in the light of England's distressing Test performances, and the International Cricket Conference attempted to bridge the ever-widening black-white divide over South Africa in the wake of the cancellation of England's tour of India.

At the risk of being overhauled by any decisions that may have been taken in the meantime, I will tell you what I think would be the best way for English cricket to achieve its twin objectives of creating the best possible environment for the development of Test cricketers and at the same time providing the levels of entertainment that attract the crowds and, consequently, the money to run the game.

But first let me give you my personal view of the seemingly insoluble South African problem which is not really a cricketing issue at all but a political one. Whatever the cricket authorities or cricketers themselves, through their professional association, decide, the ultimate decision is in the hands of the politicians – as it was when the Indian Government refused to grant visas to England players who had been to South Africa.

In all honesty, I cannot see that English cricketers who go out to South Africa to coach and play during our winter are doing any harm at all. In fact, since forty per cent of them coach only black and coloured players, I think that they are doing quite a bit of good. But we have to accept that we are dealing with politicians who believe that any involvement with South Africa is totally wrong.

My suggestion, for what it is worth, is that young players or bread-and-butter county cricketers who want to go out there to earn a living and try to improve their game in the winter should be allowed to go. But, once they achieve Test status, then, perhaps, they should have to find alternative employment elsewhere or risk being banned from international cricket. I suppose you can understand the politicians' argument that if the top players do go and play in South Africa they can be said to be giving comfort to the sporting population out there which, they say, is contrary to the spirit of the Gleneagles Agreement.

This is the only compromise that I can think of which would be fair to the lesser players and, if still not fair to the Test stars, something which they could accept and live with. At least the Test players have a lot more money coming in and, if they are not on tour, they can always get a winter job in Australia or New Zealand because of their name.

Yet I do wish the other Test-playing countries would realise how desperate some of our young professional cricketers are for winter work. They do not have that many alternatives. They cannot pick and choose. They are ready to go anywhere to do a bit of coaching and keep themselves off the dole, and I sometimes wonder whether the other countries could not do more to help the situation.

Look at the West Indies, for instance. They have banned all overseas players from playing in the Caribbean, whether they have been to South Africa or not. And that kind of thing takes a bit of swallowing by our Cricketers' Association which does not just represent English cricketers but every player in county cricket – including quite a few West Indians. I am sure that they feel the same way about it as we do, but it is their cricket boards and their governments who make the decisions and we are powerless against them.

So much for politics. Now for more fiscal matters which I am afraid are behind my biggest fear for the future as far as county cricket is concerned. Money is always an emotional topic and I know that some people believe that professional sportsmen are obsessed by it. But since I am in the process of organising my testimonial year in 1989 the subject of benefits is very much on my mind.

My concern is that because of the huge sums some players have accumulated in recent years – and I am not just talking about Mike Gatting and Allan Lamb, who had highly publicised benefits in 1988, but plenty of others before them – the tax-man is becoming so interested that the traditional system of rewarding crick- eters for their long service and loyalty is being ques- tioned. And if the worse comes to the worst and benefits are abolished altogether it could destroy the very concept of county cricket.

You may think that I have an axe to grind because I have already had one benefit in 1980 and now I have been awarded a testimonial – and you would probably be right. Yet I would defend the benefit system for the good of county cricket itself because if it does disappear I can envisage a time when players are not going to stay with one county throughout their brief careers – and I do mean brief because most are over long before they reach my age – but will go to the county offering them the highest wages.

Looking further into my crystal ball, I can even foresee a soccer-style transfer system with the wealthier clubs paying fees to snap up all the best players. That would eventually lead to a super league in which the top clubs would play each other twice, a lower division with promotion and relegation and, inevitably, one or two clubs dropping out altogether and going into the Minor Counties.

Fanciful? A gross exaggeration? Maybe – but the threat is there and it is tragic that it has appeared at a time when we are just beginning to get more talented sportsmen taking up cricket as a career rather than football. When I first started playing, there were people around the Essex scene like Bobby Moore, Geoff Hurst, Jim Standen and Eddie Presland who were all good cricketers but who made soccer their first choice for a career. You could not blame them because there was so much more money to be earned in football, but in recent years players like them have realised that if they can reach the top at cricket and play for England the financial rewards are there.

For the ordinary county cricketer, though, a benefit towards the end of his career is still the great incentive. In 1988, the average wage for capped players was still no more than £10,000 a season and at many counties they were getting considerably less than that. (David Lawrence, for example, said that in 1988, the year when he was picked to play for England, he was getting a basic £9,500 from Gloucestershire!) So, for most of them, a benefit is the only chance they have of buying the kind of house they want to spend the rest of their lives in without having too hefty a mortgage to pay.

In that respect, players in the Home Counties have to work even harder than their counterparts in other parts of the country to achieve their ambitions. And, having already had a benefit myself, I must admit that I find it very embarrassing having to go back to the same people and ask them to put their hands in their pockets yet again.

It says much for the people who support cricket and cricketers that they could not be nicer about it. They do it with a smile on their face, they make you feel at ease and they do not even seem to worry about it. It seems to be their way of showing their love for the game, their appreciation of the enjoyment that they have over the years and their desire to give something back to the players.

Yet, grateful as we all are for their wonderful support, it is still an embarrassment and I am pleased that, as the benefit system comes under scrutiny, the more forward-looking counties, Essex among them, are moving towards the establishment of some kind of insurance or pension scheme which could not only replace benefits but at the same time allay my genuine fears about wholesale movement of players in the future.

But what about my hopes? Well, like everyone else connected with Essex, I was opposed to the introduction of four-day cricket in the Britannic Assurance County Championship because it was not in our own interests. We play on so many grounds in our endeavour to be the fulcrum of cricket for the whole of Essex, rather than just a county club, that eight home games in a programme of sixteen four-day championship matches is not enough to go round. Peter Edwards, our secretary-manager who knows about these things, estimated that it would cost us more than £100,000 in lost revenue and that is money that English cricket, not just Essex cricket, cannot afford to lose.

Having said that, I must confess that the four-day cricket we played as an experiment in 1988 was far better than I thought it would be and, if it is in the wider interests of the game, I would now go along with it. We may have to change the points system a little so that sides will not just bat on into the second day for the sake of batting on and therefore bore the crowds by not making too much effort to score some runs. But the general principle of providing better conditions to produce more Test players seems to be a sound one – especially if they are given better pitches to play on.

As for the one-day game, I would like to see it standardised to fifty-five overs – with the exception of the Sunday League, now sponsored by Refuge Assurance. It would mean starting in the morning and I do not believe that the paying public want that. They want to do whatever they do on a Sunday morning, they want to have their Sunday lunch and they want to turn up at the ground at 2 o'clock, and I would be loath to change that.

There are also plenty of people, self-styled purists who do not bother to watch it anyway, or at least they say they don't, who tell us that it is not cricket at all ... and I would accept that argument to a degree. But it is fun to play (OK, it is hard work but it *is* fun), it brings in the crowds and it brings in a lot of money to the clubs. So I would now go all the way and make it a different form of cricket altogether by turning it into a real, spectacular, family entertainment with coloured clothing, white balls, black sightscreens, cheer-leaders and all the razzmatazz that we see in American sport.

I would make changes in the other competitions, too, although nothing quite as dramatic. The Benson and Hedges Cup should become a league, played on Saturdays with the four-day championship matches taking place in midweek when they would be easier to sell to sponsors – always providing that it did not increase the travelling, which is becoming a nightmare for county cricketers, especially on Friday nights.

That would leave the NatWest Trophy to continue as the premier knockout tournament but to be played over fifty-five overs rather than sixty. I know that the NatWest has been a sixty-overs competition ever since its inception as the Gillette Cup, and has produced some memorable matches, but it really is hard work for the bowlers getting through 120 overs in a day. I think that fifty-five overs are enough to produce a proper game of cricket with fortunes fluctuating between bat and ball and from one side to the other.

People are always telling us that in the old days they had no trouble bowling twenty overs in an hour, but I have to tell them that in the old days they did not change the field anything like as much as we do now. They did not have fielding circles, for a start, which have brought about a great improvement in the one-day game but which has done nothing to speed up the over-rate.

The fact that you must have four men inside the circle in the first place means that you have to take more care and therefore spend more time setting your fields. And, in the Essex side at any rate, any bowler caught running in to bowl without counting them is in trouble from Keith Fletcher, who always says: "I've got enough on my mind without having to make sure there are four in the circle."

Nor in the old days did the captain go over to a bowler in the middle of an over and say: "Right, we're going to change the line of attack against this batsman. Instead of what you've been bowling, I want you to bowl a full length on leg stump with six men on the onside. But we'll revert to what you were doing before for the other guy."

In that situation, the field may have to change after every ball if the batsmen are scoring runs and it can take an awful long time to get through an over. But it can hardly be boring. The players are not just strolling around. They are running from position to position. The bowlers are not sauntering in from third man and handing their sweaters to the umpire before walking back to bowl. They are throwing them to mid-on and getting smartly back to their marks. It is all action and there is obviously a lot of thought going into it. And if that is happening I do not see the need to worry too much about over-rates.

Obviously we have to get through the required number of overs to be bowled in the day but it should be left to the umpires to say: "Come on, get a move on – or else!" It should not be for somebody sitting behind a desk at Lord's to pontificate: "In the old days we used to bowl twenty overs an hour so you should be able to bowl eighteen."

Test cricket is different. I know from personal experience how captains will deliberately slow the game down to suit their own purposes. When we were in India, for instance, Keith Fletcher was criticised for emulating the opposition's time-wasting tactics, but when his bowlers were having to wait for minutes on end at the end of their run because the batsmen were not ready it was hardly his fault. It should really be up to the umpires to keep things moving but if they cannot or will not do it or if teams cannot or will not respond there should be a fining system like the one operating in the County Championship to make sure that sides do bowl the required number of overs. I must admit it that it has worked reasonably well in the championship – although I still do not think we need it.

Whatever we do about the cricket of the future, however, it will all be to no avail without the cricketers of the future. And Jonathan Agnew, who has taken a job as Leicestershire's cricket development officer during the winter months, told me recently that less than twenty-five per cent of English boys are now being offered the chance to play cricket at school – and that figure includes those at public schools. And I can believe him.

I have noticed that in the London area particularly, although I believe it is much the same everywhere else; schools are just not playing cricket any more. I do not know whether it is because the masters are not interested these days but, if it is, then I find that very sad since it was only through the keenness of one or two of mine that I was launched on my cricket career.

When I was in South Africa, I coached at a large school where the boys had no choice. They played cricket in the summer and rugby in the winter and it did not seem to do them any harm at all. To my mind, team games build character, teach self-discipline and provide healthy exercise – and, from what I saw out there, they also produce quite a few useful cricketers and rugby players.

Here, the burden of nurturing and encouraging young cricketers has been passing from the schools to the clubs over the past ten years or so, and I think the clubs have done a very good job. But it is not quite the same. It is not so easy for boys to find friends who are already in a club, to go and join themselves or even to pay the subscriptions. They have got to make the effort and that is not like it used to be at school when everybody played.

I would like to see those days return but I doubt whether they ever will – and, to make matters worse, many clubs are now struggling financially and finding it difficult to maintain their youth sections with the result that only the best and most committed of the young players survive.

Fortunately the more enlightened and progressive counties have recognised the situation and set up their own coaching networks which may not give every boy the chance to play the game, regardless of their level of ability, but should at least make sure that the good players come through. Essex, I am pleased to say, were one of the first in the field and are now far more geared up to finding youngsters of twelve years old and upwards.

Not that we are neglecting the schools, by any means. Only recently, Tom Pearce, president of both Essex County Cricket Club and the Essex County Schools Cricket Association, sent out a letter inviting members of the former to become vice-presidents of the latter in which he spelled out the situation perfectly.

"Whatever other reasons may be advanced for the decline in standards at the highest level of English cricket," wrote Mr Pearce, "the most significant by far is the calibre of people coming into the game at the bottom end, and we have a responsibility to ensure that our best young cricketers are encouraged to stay in the game and that they are offered the best possible opportunities to develop their skills.

"Just as important as the unearthing of youthful talent is the maintaining of school and district matches which effectively provide the feed stock for cricket at all levels throughout the county."

Some counties are better off than others, of course, and Essex are among the lucky ones. Being a large county close to London, we have a large catchment area and we have invested the profits from our seasons of success into an indoor school at Chelmsford and other youth coaching schemes and junior sides that should ensure a steady supply of cricketers in the future.

In fact we may well be producing players surplus to our

own requirements because not all of them will be able to get into the first team. I can see a time when counties such as Essex and some of the other bigger ones like Yorkshire and Lancashire finish up supplying cricketers to clubs like Leicestershire and Northamptonshire, which seem to struggle to produce their own home-grown talent. It would take away some of the local flavour of county cricket but I cannot see too much wrong with it if good young players are given opportunities that they would not get otherwise.

Not everybody can be as lucky as I was to go straight into the Essex side and stay there for more than twenty years . . . but whether I will be lucky enough to be given the chance to give something back to the club when I retire in the not too distant future remains to be seen. Jobs in county cricket are few and far between, and with Keith Fletcher taking over our 2nd XI as well as keeping an eye on the first team and Ray East in charge of the Under 19s I have to be realistic. I would love to stay within the Essex set-up, but the organisation is far too professional for them to pay anybody just for the sake of having them there.

I have had offers from other counties but, while I would like to stay in the game, I am not too sure whether I would ever be able to detach myself from Essex after so many years. I suppose I might feel differently when I finally stop playing.

In the meantime, I have had a job for the past two winters which could be described as "something in the city". Bill Bateman, a slow-left-arm bowler in the Ilford side when I first started playing for them, and his partner, Steve Pinner, started a computer-based company called Security Settlements and offered me the opportunity to learn the business and see if I could get used to the City life. But, even if I do finish up in the bowler-hat brigade, I am sure that my love of the game and my fascination by it will keep me involved, whether it is as a player, an umpire or an administrator, with my club.

I have always spent quite a bit of time at Ilford – even during the winter because I play football for a local side which uses the cricket club bar – but everything has taken on a different aspect since I became chairman and discovered that there was a bit more to it than saying: "Me? Chairman? Oh yes, that'll be fine."

I am also beginning to find out that there are a lot of people who want to play cricket but are not prepared to do any of the work that is necessary to make it possible – which I am sure will ring a bell with anybody involved in club cricket in an administrative position. There are always a certain few people who do all the work and the rest who just turn up on a Saturday, play their cricket and go home. But at Ilford the situation got so bad that we faced the awful possibility of one of the most famous clubs in Essex if not the Home Counties having to fold up because no one wanted to take on the jobs of secretary and treasurer.

My old friend David Tack is now the secretary and I became more and more involved through listening to him, and sympathising with him, whenever we met for a beer and he began to moan about all the problems involved – problems which became very apparent to me when I played for Ilford a couple of times in 1988.

In the first game, the opposition did not turn up until half an hour after the scheduled start because somebody at their club had not told the players that it had been changed because of the time of year. In the second game, at home, we were all ready to take the field when we discovered that no one had brought any cricket balls with them.

Incidents like that bring it home to you very forcibly that unless people are prepared to do the work behind the scenes you are just not going to get a game of cricket at all.

And if that sort of thing happens too often even clubs as famous as Ilford can fold up very, very easily.

People like David Tack and John Polson – who served Ilford for more than fifty years as secretary and president before becoming president of the Club Cricket Conference, which was a great honour for us as well as him – think that my name might help to stir up a bit more interest.

But it is not quite the same popping into Valentine's Park to have a pint and watch a bit of cricket when somebody taps you on the shoulder and says: "Can I just have a quick word?"

"Yes, what is it?"

"They've run out of paper in the ladies' loo."

It is a long way from the Test match scene . . . but then I could not have had one without the other.

J. K. LEVER
CAREER STATISTICS
Compiled by Kevin Montgomery

First Class Matches: Batting and Fielding

Season	Matches	Inns.	N.O.	Runs	H.S.	Av.	100s	50s	0s	Ct
1967	14	21	4	114	28	6.70	0	0	4	4
1968	26	28	16	99	24*	8.25	0	0	5	15
1969	22	26	9	124	20*	7.29	0	0	7	16
1970	16	17	11	189	91	31.50	0	1	1	2
1971	23	27	15	169	37*	14.08	0	0	2	11
1972	22	19	7	143	38*	11.91	0	0	5	11
1972–73 South Africa	5	8	3	39	13	7.80	0	0	1	2
1973	23	24	11	156	22*	12.00	0	0	3	14
1973–74 South Africa	6	4	3	20	9*	20.00	0	0	0	2
1974	21	19	13	91	19*	15.16	0	0	0	8
1975	22	29	14	138	35	9.20	0	0	3	7
1976	22	24	10	178	31*	12.71	0	0	2	6
1976–77 India	10	12	2	150	53	15.00	0	1	1	6
1976–77 Sri Lanka	1	—	—	—	—	—	—	—	—	—
1976–77 Australia	1	2	0	15	11	7.50	0	0	0	0
1977	19	17	4	73	11	5.61	0	0	2	8
1977–78 Sri Lanka	1	—	—	—	—	—	—	—	—	—
1977–78 Pakistan	4	4	2	37	33*	18.50	0	0	1	1
1977–78 New Zealand	4	4	0	28	18	7.00	0	0	0	3
1978	22	15	7	85	30	10.62	0	0	2	9
1978–79 Australia	6	7	0	67	28	9.57	0	0	0	0
1979	21	16	6	81	14	8.10	0	0	0	3
1979–80 Australia	6	6	2	54	22	13.50	0	0	2	3
1979–80 India	1	1	0	21	21	21.00	0	0	0	1
1980	21	21	10	123	18*	11.18	0	0	2	6
1980–81 India	1	2	0	100	73	50.00	0	1	0	0
1981	22	20	4	147	21	9.18	0	0	3	6
1981–82 India	7	5	1	34	16	8.50	0	0	0	1
1981–82 Sri Lanka	1	1	0	2	2	2.00	0	0	0	1
1981–82 South Africa	4	5	3	41	10*	20.50	0	0	0	0
1982	18	19	3	89	22*	5.56	0	0	6	5
1982–83 South Africa	8	11	1	67	19	6.70	0	0	0	1
1983	18	17	3	211	44	15.07	0	0	0	7
1984	24	22	7	182	37	12.13	0	0	4	10
1984–85 South Africa	4	6	3	50	16	16.66	0	0	0	0
1985	23	23	9	193	24*	13.78	0	0	2	8
1986	23	27	6	199	38	9.47	0	0	4	1
1987	15	9	2	60	18	8.57	0	0	2	4
1988	13	13	1	53	20	4.42	0	0	5	2
Career Total	520	531	192	3622	91	10.68	0	3	69	184

First Class Matches continued

Matches in Great Britain

For Essex:	Matches	Inns.	N.O.	Runs	H.S.	Av.	100s	50s	0s	Ct
Championship (1967–88)	405	413	161	2575	91	10.22	0	1	57	151
Other Matches (1967–87)	29	23	7	199	37*	12.44	0	0	5	6
Total for Essex	434	436	168	2774	91	10.35	0	1	62	157
England Tests (1977–86)	6	9	2	49	15	7.00	0	0	1	3
England Test Trial (1976)	1	—	—	—	—	—	—	—	—	1
The Rest Test Trials (1973–74)	2	1	0	18	18	18.00	0	0	0	0
England Under 25 (1971)	1	2	0	7	7	3.50	0	0	1	0
Young England (1973)	1	1	1	9	9*	—	0	0	0	0
M.C.C. (1973–79)	3	2	0	32	30	16.00	0	0	0	1
D. H. Robin's XI (1974)	1	—	—	—	—	—	—	—	—	—
International XI (1975)	1	2	1	8	6*	8.00	0	0	0	1
Total in Great Britain	450	453	172	2897	91	10.31	0	1	64	163

Matches in Australia

	Matches	Inns.	N.O.	Runs	H.S.	Av.	100s	50s	0s	Ct
England (1977–80)	3	6	0	73	22	12.17	0	0	0	1
England XI (1978–80)	10	9	2	63	28	9.00	0	0	2	2
Total in Australia	13	15	2	136	28	10.46	0	0	2	3

Matches in South Africa

	Matches	Inns.	N.O.	Runs	H.S.	Av.	100s	50s	0s	Ct
D. H. Robin's XI (1973)	11	12	6	59	13	9.83	0	0	1	4
Unofficial Tests (1982)	3	4	2	31	10*	15.50	0	0	0	0
SAB English XI	1	1	1	10	10*	—	0	0	0	0
Natal (1982–85)	12	17	4	117	19	9.00	0	0	0	1
Total in South Africa	27	34	13	217	19	10.33	0	0	1	5

Matches in New Zealand

	Matches	Inns.	N.O.	Runs	H.S.	Av.	100s	50s	0s	Ct
England (1978)	1	1	0	1	1	1.00	0	0	0	0
England XI (1978)	3	3	0	27	18	9.00	0	0	0	3
Total in New Zealand	4	4	0	28	18	7.00	0	0	0	3

Matches in India

	Matches	Inns.	N.O.	Runs	H.S.	Av.	100s	50s	0s	Ct
England (1976–81)	8	11	1	146	53	14.60	0	1	0	6
M.C.C./England XI (1976–82)	10	7	2	59	17	11.80	0	0	1	2
Overseas XI (1980–81)	1	2	0	100	73	50.00	0	1	0	0
Total in India	19	20	3	305	73	17.94	0	2	1	8

First Class Matches continued

Matches in Pakistan

	Matches	Inns.	N.O.	Runs	H.S.	Av.	100s	50s	0s	Ct
England (1977–78)	3	4	2	37	33*	18.50	0	0	1	1
England XI (1977)	1	—	—	—	—	—	—	—	—	—
Total in Pakistan	4	4	2	37	33*	18.50	0	0	1	1

Matches in Sri Lanka

	Matches	Inns.	N.O.	Runs	H.S.	Av.	100s	50s	0s	Ct
M.C.C./England XI (1977–82)	2	1	0	2	2	2.00	0	0	0	1
D. H. Robin's XI (1977)	1	—	—	—	—	—	—	—	—	—
Total in Sri Lanka	3	1	0	2	2	2.00	0	0	0	1

Highest Score: 91 for Essex v. Glamorgan at Sophia Gardens, Cardiff, 1970.
Best season: 211 runs (av. 15.07) in 1983.

First Class Matches: Bowling

Season	6bO.	8bO.	Mdns	Runs	Wkts	Av.	5WI.	10WM	Best
1967	315.2	—	65	822	27	30.44	1	0	5–66
1968	623	—	159	1539	50	30.78	0	0	4–49
1969	521	—	112	1401	62	22.59	1	0	6–72
1970	356.1	—	65	1078	31	34.77	0	0	4–32
1971	528.3	—	95	1535	68	22.57	2	0	7–90
1972	535.2	—	110	1399	61	22.93	4	0	5–42
1972–73 South Africa	147	—	41	348	16	21.75	0	0	3–20
1973	652	—	155	1678	63	26.63	2	0	5–54
1973–74 South Africa	195.5	—	41	528	20	26.40	2	0	6–117
1974	479.2	—	78	1349	31	43.51	0	0	3–38
1975	704.1	—	155	1807	85	21.25	2	0	5–11
1976	682.1	—	148	1909	70	27.27	4	0	8–127
1976–77 India	270.4	—	56	672	44	15.27	2	1	7–46
1976–77 Sri Lanka	—	30	4	95	5	19.00	0	0	4–50
1976–77 Australia	—	33	2	131	4	32.75	0	0	2–36
1977	504.4	—	123	1303	58	22.46	4	0	6–34
1977–78 Ski Lanka	—	13	3	24	1	24.00	0	0	1–24
1977–78 Pakistan	—	84.6	18	255	10	25.50	0	0	3–11
1977–78 New Zealand	—	107.4	22	321	19	16.89	1	0	5–59
1978	681.1	—	162	1610	106	15.18	9	1	7–32
1978–79 Australia	—	118.1	18	377	13	29.00	0	0	4–28
1979	700	—	166	1834	106	17.30	8	2	8–49
1979–80 Australia	192.4	—	50	475	12	39.58	0	0	4–111
1979–80 India	43.2	—	5	147	4	36.75	0	0	3–65
1980	591	—	126	1703	60	28.28	3	0	6–121
1980–81 India	42	—	13	112	4	28.00	0	0	2–39
1981	680.5	—	149	2049	80	25.61	4	1	8–49

First Class Matches continued

Season	6bO.	8bO.	Mdns	Runs	Wkts	Av.	5WI.	10WM	Best
1981–82 India	189	—	39	602	17	35.41	1	0	5–100
1981–82 Sri Lanka	25	—	6	62	3	20.66	0	0	2–45
1981–82 South Africa	107	—	25	335	11	30.45	1	0	6–86
1982	543.5	—	112	1683	72	23.37	5	1	6–48
1982–83 South Africa	314.4	—	67	941	23	40.91	1	0	5–79
1983	569	—	137	1726	106	16.28	8	3	7–55
1984	874.5	—	195	2550	116	21.98	8	3	8–37
1984–85 South Africa	179	—	52	432	14	30.85	0	0	4–58
1985	720.3	—	188	1995	77	25.90	6	0	6–47
1986	638.1	—	154	1990	70	28.42	3	0	6–57
1987	396	—	99	1079	34	31.73	2	0	5–59
1988	422.4	—	90	1120	43	26.05	0	0	4–61
Career Total	14425.5	386.3	3305	41016	1696	24.18	84	12	8–37

Matches in Great Britain

For Essex:	6bO.	8bO.	Mdns	Runs	Wkts	Av.	5WI.	10WM	Best
Championship	11569	—	2528	32183	1357	23.72	72	11	8–37
Other Matches	699.3	—	203	1732	90	19.24	4	0	7–63
Total for Essex	12268.3	—	2731	33915	1447	23.44	76	11	8–37

	6bO.	8bO.	Mdns	Runs	Wkts	Av.	5WI.	10WM	Best
England Tests	189.5	—	48	562	14	40.14	0	0	4–64
England Test Trial	18	—	4	57	0	—	0	0	—
The Rest Test Trials	69	—	12	182	3	60.66	0	0	2–39
England Under 25	25	—	7	63	2	31.50	0	0	2–19
Young England	24	—	9	49	0	—	0	0	—
M.C.C.	98.2	—	28	266	8	33.25	0	0	4–92
D. H. Robin's XI	13	—	1	29	2	14.50	0	0	2–18
International XI	14	—	3	36	0	—	0	0	—
Total in Great Britain	12719.4	—	2843	35159	1476	23.82	76	11	8–37

Matches in Australia

	6bO.	8bO.	Mdns	Runs	Wkts	Av.	5WI.	10WM	Best
England	60.4	48.1	22	308	13	23.69	0	0	4–28
England XI	132	103	48	675	16	42.19	0	0	2–25
Total in Australia	192.4	151.1	70	983	29	33.90	0	0	4–28

CAREER STATISTICS

First Class Matches continued

Matches in South Africa

	6bO.	8bO.	Mdns	Runs	Wkts	Av.	5WI.	10WM	Best
D. H. Robin's XI	342.5	—	82	876	36	24.33	2	0	6–117
Unofficial Tests	106.4	—	25	335	11	30.45	1	0	6–86
SAB English XI	0.2	—	0	0	0	—	0	0	—
Natal	493.4	—	119	1373	37	37.11	1	0	5–79
Total in South Africa	943.3	—	226	2584	84	30.76	4	0	6–86

Matches in New Zealand

	6bO.	8bO.	Mdns	Runs	Wkts	Av.	5WI.	10WM	Best
England	—	51	9	155	5	31.00	0	0	3–96
England XI	—	56.4	13	166	14	11.85	1	0	5–59
Total in New Zealand	—	107.4	22	321	19	16.89	1	0	5–59

Matches in India

	6bO.	8bO.	Mdns	Runs	Wkts	Av.	5WI.	10WM	Best
England	266	—	50	731	37	19.76	3	1	7–46
M.C.C./England XI	237	—	50	690	28	24.64	0	0	4–51
Overseas XI	42	—	13	112	4	28.00	0	0	2–39
Total in India	545	—	113	1533	69	22.22	3	1	7–46

Matches in Pakistan

	6bO.	8bO.	Mdns	Runs	Wkts	Av.	5WI.	10WM	Best
England	—	67.6	14	195	4	48.75	0	0	2–47
England XI	—	17	4	60	6	10.00	0	0	3–11
Total in Pakistan	—	84.6	18	255	10	25.50	0	0	3–11

Matches in Sri Lanka

	6bO.	8bO.	Mdns	Runs	Wkts	Av.	5WI.	10WM	Best
M.C.C./England XI	25	30	10	157	8	19.63	0	0	4–50
D. H. Robin's XI	—	13	3	24	1	24.00	0	0	1–24
Total in Sri Lanka	25	43	13	181	9	20.11	0	0	4–50

Best bowling: 8–37 for Essex v. Gloucestershire at Bristol, 1984.
Best match analysis: 13–87 for Essex v. Warwickshire at Edgbaston, 1979.
Best season: 116 wickets (av. 21.98) in 1984.

179

Test Matches for England

Batting and Fielding

	Matches	Inns.	N.O.	Runs	H.S.	Av.	100s	50s	0s	Ct
v. Australia (1977–80)	6	10	0	97	22	9.70	0	0	0	3
v. New Zealand (1978)	1	1	0	1	1	1.00	0	0	0	0
v. India (1976–86)	10	14	3	152	53	13.82	0	1	1	6
v. Pakistan (1977–78)	3	4	2	37	33*	18.50	0	0	1	1
v. West Indies (1980)	1	2	0	19	15	9.50	0	0	0	1
Test Career Total	21	31	5	306	53	11.77	0	1	2	11

Highest score: 53 v. India at New Delhi, 1976–77.

Bowling

	6bO.	8bO.	Mdns	Runs	Wkts	Av.	5WI.	10WM	Best
v. Australia	135.4	48.1	44	505	18	28.06	0	0	4–28
v. New Zealand	—	51	9	155	5	31.00	0	0	3–96
v. India	352.5	—	69	995	45	22.11	3	1	7–46
v. Pakistan	—	67.6	14	195	4	48.75	0	0	2–47
v. West Indies	28	—	7	101	1	101.00	0	0	1–76
Test Career Total	516.3	166.7	143	1951	73	26.73	3	1	7–46

Best bowling: 7–46 v. India at New Delhi, 1976–77.
Best match analysis: 10–70 v. India at New Delhi, 1976–77.

Limited Overs Cricket: Batting and Fielding

	Matches	Inns.	N.O.	Runs	H.S.	Av.	100s	50s	0s	Ct
Gillette Cup (1968–80)	24	17	10	49	8	7.00	0	0	1	3
National Westminster Bank Trophy (1981–88)	19	9	8	45	15*	45.00	0	0	0	0
Combined	43	26	18	94	15*	11.75	0	0	1	3
Benson and Hedges Cup (1972–88)	85	26	18	104	13	13.00	0	0	2	18
John Player League (1969–86)	252	101	62	382	23	9.79	0	0	9	60
Refuge Assurance League (1987–88)	24	12	6	20	6*	3.33	0	0	4	10
Combined	276	113	68	402	23	8.93	0	0	13	70

Highest scores:
Gillette Cup: 8 v. Hertfordshire at Hitchin, 1976.
National Westminster Bank: 15* v. Surrey at Chelmsford, 1984.
John Player League: 23 v. Worcestershire at Worcester, 1974.
Refuge Assurance League: 6* v. Somerset at Taunton, 1987.
Benson and Hedges Cup: 13 v. Lancashire at Chelmsford, 1984.

One-day internationals

For England in Prudential Trophy:

	Matches	Inns.	N.O.	Runs	H.S.	Av.	100s	50s	0s	Ct
v. Australia (1977)	3	3	1	30	27*	15.00	0	0	0	0
v. West Indies (1976–80)	4	3	1	7	6	3.50	0	0	0	4
v. New Zealand (1978)	2	1	1	5	5*	—	0	0	0	0
v. Pakistan (1978)	1	—	—	—	—	—	—	—	—	—
Total	10	7	3	42	27*	10.50	0	0	0	4

For England in Australian Benson and Hedges Cup

	Matches	Inns.	N.O.	Runs	H.S.	Av.	100s	50s	0s	Ct
v. Australia (1979–80)	5	1	0	1	1	1.00	0	0	0	0
v. West Indies (1980)	1	1	0	11	11	11.00	0	0	0	0
Total	6	2	0	12	11	6.00	0	0	0	0

Other one day internationals for England

	Matches	Inns.	N.O.	Runs	H.S.	Av.	100s	50s	0s	Ct
v. India (1981–82)	3	—	—	—	—	—	—	—	—	1
v. Sri Lanka (1982)	1	1	1	2	2*	—	0	0	0	0
v. Pakistan (1977–78)	2	1	0	0	0	—	0	0	1	1
Career Total	22	11	4	56	27*	8.00	0	0	0	6

Highest score: 27* v. Australia at Edgbaston, 1977.

For Natal in South Africa

	Matches	Inns.	N.O.	Runs	H.S.	Av.	100s	50s	0s	Ct
Datsun Shield (1982–83)	3	2	0	6	4	3.00	0	0	0	1
Benson and Hedges (1982–84)	9	5	3	38	19	19.00	0	0	0	1
Nissan Shield (1983)	1	—	—	—	—	—	—	—	—	1

Highest score:
Datsun Shield: 4 v. Western Province at Durban, 1982.
Benson and Hedges: 19 v. Eastern Province at Pietermaritzburg, 1983.

Limited Overs Cricket: Bowling

	Overs	Mdns.	Runs	Wkts.	Av.	4wI.	Runs/ Over	Balls/ Wkt	Best
Gillette Cup	255.4	56	684	44	15.54	5	2.68	34.86	5–8
National Westminster Bank Trophy	182.2	48	493	26	18.96	1	2.70	42.08	4–39
Combined	438	104	1177	70	16.81	6	2.69	37.54	5–8
Benson and Hedges Cup	852.1	163	2614	143	18.28	8	3.07	35.76	5–13
John Player League	1760.2	198	6430	344	18.69	15	3.65	30.70	5–13

Limited Overs Cricket continued

	Overs	Mdns.	Runs	Wkts.	Av.	4wI.	Runs/ Over	Balls/ Wkt	Best
Refuge Assurance League	170.5	11	800	21	38.10	1	4.68	48.80	4–28
Combined	1931.1	209	7230	365	19.81	16	3.74	31.75	5–13

Best bowling:
Gillette Cup: 5–8 v. Middlesex at Westcliff, 1972.
National Westminster Bank: 4–39 v. Worcestershire at Chelmsford, 1987.
John Player League: 5–13 v. Glamorgan at Ebbw Vale, 1975.
Refuge Assurance League: 4–28 v. Glamorgan at Neath, 1987.
Benson and Hedges Cup: 5–13 v. Middlesex at Lord's, 1985.

One day internationals

For England in Prudential Trophy

	Overs	Mdns.	Runs	Wkts.	Av.	4wI.	Runs/ Over	Balls/ Wkt	Best
v. Australia	31	3	117	7	16.71	1	3.77	26.57	4–29
v. West Indies	37	7	154	3	51.33	0	4.16	74.00	2–57
v. New Zealand	18	2	53	1	53.00	0	2.94	108.00	1–28
v. Pakistan	7	1	17	0	—	0	2.43	—	—
Total	93	13	341	11	31.00	1	3.67	50.73	4–29

For England in Australian Benson and Hedges Cup

	Overs	Mdns.	Runs	Wkts.	Av.	4wI.	Runs/ Over	Balls/ Wkt	Best
v. Australia	29+	4	92	6	15.33	0	3.17	35.67	3–51
v. West Indies	10	1	54	0	—	0	5.40	—	—
+ 20 of these 8 ball overs									
Total	39	5	146	6	24.33	0	3.74	39.00	3–51

Other one day internationals for England

	Overs	Mdns.	Runs	Wkts.	Av.	4wI.	Runs/ Over	Balls/ Wkt	Best
v. India	27	0	132	0	—	—	4.89	—	—
v. Sri Lanka	9	0	51	2	25.50	0	5.67	27.00	2–51
v. Pakistan 8 ball overs	13	2	43	5	8.60	0	3.31	20.80	3–18
Career Total	181+	20	713	24	29.71	1	3.94	48.00	4–29
+ 33 of these 8 ball overs									

Best bowling: 4–29 v. Australia at Edgbaston, 1977.

For Natal in South Africa

	Overs	Mdns.	Runs	Wkts.	Av.	4wI.	Runs/ Over	Balls/ Wkt	Best
Datsun Shield	30.4	4	102	10	10.20	1	3.33	18.40	4–18
Benson and Hedges	76.4	7	275	10	27.50	0	3.59	46.00	3–17
Nissan Shield	9	1	40	0	—	0	4.44	—	—

Best bowling:
Datsun Shield: 4–18 v. Orange Free State at Bloemfontein, 1982.
Benson and Hedges: 3–17 v. Eastern Province at Johannesburg, 1984.

Index